The Modern Herbalist

Unlocking Ancient Wisdom for Today's Health

Legal Disclaimer!

This book is authored for informational and educational purposes only.

While the publisher and author have made every effort to provide accurate information, they make no representations or warranties of any kind, implied or express, about the contents' reliability, accuracy, completeness, availability, or suitability for all persons.

The reader assumes full responsibility for the use of the information contained herein.

The publisher and author disclaim all liability for any damage, loss, injury, or expense that may manifest from using the information in this book.

Table of Contents

Introduction

More than 80 percent of the global population depends on natural medicine to meet their basic health care requirements. It just goes to show how effective nature still is, and I think that this is a very strong sign that maybe we should listen to our forefathers.

With a basic knowledge of herbalism, it is easy to see how a leaf or root can cure sicknesses and strengthen the body and even the soul. Natural remedies are exceptional and versatile, providing comprehensive cures that the contemporary world's science might not consider. Investigations have demonstrated that ginger can help lessen muscle soreness by 25%, while aloe vera enhances burn recovery by nine days as compared to other therapies. Rather than seeing them as mere folktales, these are facts supported by research work that connects the conventional knowledge of the world to the scientific knowledge of the contemporary world.

Blending the old and the new, this book will guide you through a path of discovery where the wisdom of the past is wed with the science of the present. No one is saying that you should reject the use of drugs and hospitals, but supplementing them with ageless natural remedies is the way to go. A cup of peppermint tea can treat headaches, which has been shown to lessen tension headaches by up to 50%, or using turmeric as an anti-inflammatory that has been backed by clinical research. This fusion not only expands your healing options but also puts choices that are healthier and kinder to the body in your hands.

But as they say, power is not given to be lorded over but to be exercised with great responsibility. Herbal treatments, as effective as they are, require attention to be paid. Measures that should be taken and factors that should be considered are vital to guarantee safety and efficiency. For example, St. John's Wort is an excellent remedy for mood swings; however, it is not compatible with birth control pills and antidepressants. This book will take you through these shades so that your introduction to herbalism is well-informed and safe.

Well, are you ready for a deeper look at what nature has to offer and what is contained in its vast treasure chest? Come along, and I will tell you all about it!

Part I

Herbal Healing

Chapter 1

Nature's Medicine Cabinet

The beauty of Mother Nature is a storehouse of cure and remedy. These natural cures, which have been handed down from generation to generation, are the secret to good health and a long life. It just goes to show that with the right knowledge, anyone can harness the properties of these plants that have been used for centuries. Amidst the rapidity of modern society, the pathway to wholeness is found in reengaging with the earth's medicine chest. Take a look at what medicinal herbs are and how they can impact your life for the better.

Common Medicinal Herbs

Herbal remedies have been the basis of the healing practices for many years now. These plants contain active ingredients that make them more efficient in treating diseases than normal medicine. Take chamomile, for instance. This lowly flower is credited with having a sedative influence; thus, it is the best herb to treat insomnia and anxiety. It also has anti-inflammatory properties making it useful in easing digestion complications. Another one is echinacea, the immune system booster. Another herb that is frequently taken to prevent colds and flu, echinacea is packed with antioxidants and helps to decrease inflammation.

Lavender, which has a calming smell, is not only used for aromatherapy. This herb has multiple uses in that it can help cure headaches, lessen anxiety, and even help one get a good night's sleep. It also has antibacterial properties and is used to treat small injuries such as cuts and burns. Another must-have is peppermint, a herb that is used to soothe the tummy. It also contains menthol, which can be effective in unblocking the breathing passage and relief of muscle pain.

Turmeric also known as the golden spice, has been known to have some health benefits such as anti-inflammatory and antioxidant. It is applied in the treatment of arthritis and other digestive system diseases. In the same way, ginger, which has a spicy taste, is used to treat nausea, indigestion, and inflammation. These are just a few examples of the many herbs that can be used to benefit from their medicinal properties. When you include these herbs in your diet, it can be a way of preventing diseases and illnesses from occurring in the first place.

Growing Your Herbal Garden

Growing your herbs is a very satisfying task that adds aesthetic value to your home and improves the health of its inhabitants. The process begins with the selection of a location. Herbs require well-drained soil and a place where they will be exposed to sunlight for at least six hours per day. Regardless of the size of the garden you have, be it an extensive backyard or a tiny balcony, you can grow various herbs.

Start with simple plants such as basil, parsley, and thyme. Most of these herbs are perennial and, therefore, do not demand a lot of care. Grow them in containers or in mounds to facilitate good drainage. Irrigation is important; however, herbs require frequent water but ensure you do not flood them because it will result in root rot. A basic suggestion is to use the finger check – if the soil is dry up to the first knuckle, it is time to water.

Companion planting can also help increase the yield of your garden as well. For example, placing basil near tomatoes enhances the taste of the tomatoes and also acts as an insect repellent. This helps the herbs grow and also discourages the herbs from growing long and thin which is known as legginess. Pruning the top of the herbs not only maintains the plants but also gives you fresh clippings for use in the kitchen.

Riding the herbs with organic compost or a balanced fertilizer will guarantee that the herbs get the right nutrients. Herbs also have their requirements that must be met. Some have to be fed more often than others. As you tend to your herbal garden properly, your plants will grow healthy and continuously supply you with fresh, all-natural herbs for use in your kitchen or for making teas or remedies.

Harvesting and Preserving Herbs

Most of the herbs should be harvested when they are young and before they flower to get the best results. Ideally, it is preferred that the crops are harvested in the early morning when the dew has dried up but not at midday when the sun is scorching. This is the best time as the essential oils of the herbs are produced. Trim the herbs using a sharp scissor or pruning shears to have a clean cut, which encourages growth. Do not take more than a third of the plant at a time so that the plant can grow back again.

When harvested, herbs can either be used fresh or dried, depending on the need of the user. Drying is one of the most effective ways of preservation that man has ever employed. Secure the herbs in small bunches and dry them in a cool, well-ventilated, and dark area with little exposure to light. Make sure there is proper ventilation to avoid the formation of mold. In case you are in a hurry, you can use a dehydrator to reduce the time taken considerably. After the herbs have been dried, they should be stored in well-sealed containers in a dry, dark, and cool place to retain their strength.

Freezing is another method that can be used, especially when dealing with fresh herbs such as basil and parsley. Finely chop the herbs and pack them into ice cube trays and then pour over cold water or olive oil and freeze. This way, you can pop out a cube whenever you need to add a burst of flavor to your dishes. Herbal oils or vinegar are also effective means of preserving the properties of the herbs as well. Just put the fresh herbs in a jar, pour oil or vinegar on top, and let it steep in a cool and dark place for about a week to 2 weeks, and then strain it.

Another technique for long-term preservation is making herbal tinctures or extracts. These concentrated forms preserve the herbs in alcohol or glycerin; their effects are strong and can be applied the whole year round. With these preservation methods, you can be sure that at any given time, you will have fresh herbs from your home garden to enhance your health and well-being naturally.

Chapter 2

Herbal Remedies for Common Ailments

When was the last time you felt well? Not only the absence of disease, but an energy in your bones, a lightness in your head, and a warmth in your soul? It is quite telling that most of us have probably lost touch with the sensation of true health. In a society where everything is fast and people opt for artificial solutions, the knowledge of herbs is a healing balm. This chapter looks at the traditional cures that are in use today and examines how the modern world can incorporate them into people's daily lives.

Boosting Immunity

How frequently do we get downed by a mere flu or a cold, leaving us out of the beautiful things in life and our duties? Find out how herbs such as echinacea, elderberry, and astragalus can boost your immune system and decrease the number of days you are likely to fall sick. Using these natural remedies that have been in existence for centuries, you can be prepared against such common flu viruses, and this will make you stay healthy and active all through the year.

The Power of Prevention

It is quite startling to learn that an average adult gets infected by a cold two to three times a year. That's a lot of sniffling, sneezing, and days lost from school or work. Although it is impossible to prevent colds and flu completely, some herbs can increase immunity and minimize the occurrences of these diseases.

Key Herbs to Enhance Immunity:

- **Echinacea:** This herb is particularly famous for its ability to increase the immunity of the human body. Regular use can help prevent infections.
- **Elderberry:** Elderberry is also an antiviral agent which is rich in antioxidants and vitamins.
- **Astragalus:** Common in Chinese medicine, astragalus strengthens the body's defenses.
- **Garlic:** Garlic is known to have antibacterial and antiviral compounds, so it is good for preventing colds.
- **Ginger:** This warming herb can increase circulation and is beneficial in preventing sickness.
- **Turmeric:** It can reduce inflammation, hence boosting the immune system.

Echinacea

Echinacea, commonly known as the purple coneflower, is more than just a flower that can be admired from a distance. The roots and leaves possess chemicals that strengthen the immune system through the promotion of the growth of white blood cells, which are the body's first line of defense.

How to Use Echinacea

- **Tea**: Boil the dried leaves of echinacea and consume it as tea.
- **Tincture**: A few drops of echinacea tincture can be added to water or juice.
- **Capsules**: If one does not have time for preparation of the herbal tea, then the echinacea capsules are also available in the market.
- **Extract**: Echinacea extract can be combined with honey and taken as a syrup that has a pleasant taste.
- **Topical**: Echinacea cream can be applied to cuts and wounds to prevent infections.

Elderberry

Elderberries have been used for a long time to treat flu. Contemporary science supports this folk remedy; elderberries have anti-viral properties and can decrease the flu symptoms' duration.

Incorporating Elderberry

- **Syrup**: Elderberry syrup is a tasty way to make sure you are getting elderberries every day.
- **Gummies**: Children and grown-ups love elderberry gummies.
- **Juice**: The juice of elderberries can be mixed with other fruits in the preparation of a smoothie or taken on its own.
- **Jam**: It is possible to get a tasty meal of elderberry jam on toast and get a cure for the flu at the same time.
- **Wine**: Elderberry wine is another method by which one can take elderberries.

Astragalus

Another powerful herb is the root of Astragalus, which is known for its immune-enhancing effect. It should be noted that it is particularly effective in the prevention of respiratory infections.

Astragalus Preparation:

- **Broth**: Astragalus root can be taken in soups and broths and is very easy to add to one's diet.
- **Powder**: Astragalus powder can be added to smoothies or simply sprinkled on foods.
- **Capsules**: Similar to echinacea, astragalus is also available in capsules for easier consumption.
- **Tea**: The root can be prepared as an Astragalus tea by boiling the root in water.
- **Extract**: Astragalus extract can be consumed by mixing it with water or juice to boost energy levels in the body.

Digestive Ease

Gastrointestinal problems are an inconvenience and can affect one's well-being through discomfort. Peppermint, ginger, and chamomile are some of the most effective herbs that should be used for gentle treatment of your gut and digestion purposes. Embrace these natural remedies to enable the body to have a calm and balanced digestion.

Digestive Health

Gastrointestinal problems are a common complaint and are experienced by millions of people all over the globe. Whether it's occasional discomfort in the tummy or long-term issues like IBS, herbs can provide natural and gentle relief to the tummy. Digestive health is essential to the well-being of an individual because it enables the body to break down food and expel waste.

Essential Herbs for Digestive Health

- **Peppermint**: It is known for its cool and calming relief to the digestive system.
- **Ginger**: An effective anti-inflammatory that can help get rid of nausea and enhance digestion.

- **Chamomile**: Sometimes, they are taken to help with stomach cramps and to make one relax.
- **Fennel**: Reduces cases of swelling and formation of gases in the stomach.
- **Licorice Root**: This herb helps in the healing of ulcers and decreases inflammation.
- Dandelion: Helps to improve digestion and liver function.

Peppermint

It is well known that peppermint has been used for centuries in the treatment of digestive problems. It contains menthol that has a calming effect on the stomach lining, thus making it suitable for IBS and indigestion.

Ways to Use Peppermint

- **Tea**: Another natural treatment for digestive problems is peppermint tea.
- **Oil**: The peppermint oil can be diluted and then applied topically on the abdomen.
- **Capsules**: Peppermint capsules are coated with enteric so that they dissolve and release the contents in the intestines only.
- **Fresh Leaves**: The fresh peppermint leaves are good for chewing to cure bad breath and aid in digestion.
- **Inhalation**: Inhaling peppermint steam can help in reducing nausea.

Ginger

Ginger is a popular spice that can be used in foods and has many health benefits, especially regarding digestion. It is especially effective against nausea, whether from motion sickness, morning sickness in pregnancy, or nausea caused by chemotherapy.

Incorporating Ginger

- **Tea**: Ginger tea can be prepared by boiling sliced ginger in hot water and it is advised to take fresh ginger tea.
- **Candied Ginger**: A snack that is equally beneficial in treating nausea.
- **Powder**: Ginger powder is best used in smoothies, soups, and baking products.
- **Juice**: Fresh ginger juice can be prepared and taken with honey and lemon as a very effective remedy.
- **Capsules**: For a more potent ginger experience, you can take ginger capsules.

Chamomile

Chamomile is not just an herbal tea that one takes before sleeping. It is a good medication for treating problems related to the digestive system due to its anti-inflammatory and antispasmodic effects.

Chamomile Usage:

- **Tea**: Chamomile tea is a mild yet potent treatment for stomach aches and other digestion issues.
- **Tincture**: This is where a few drops of chamomile tincture will come in handy and help to resolve the issue quickly.
- **Compress**: Warm chamomile compress can be applied warmly on the stomach to help reduce cramps and discomfort.
- **Bath**: You can relax the body and soothe the digestive system by adding chamomile to the bath.
- **Inhalation**: Steam inhalation with chamomile is used for relieving mental stress and for the relaxation of the digestive system.

Stress Relief

Stress is one of the sneakiest killers that slowly and gradually steal away our happiness and health. This is a problem that every person experiences and almost none of them deal with it properly. Thus, herbs can be used to achieve a state of mind and body that is free from stress and tension. This section brings to the reader's notice some of the less well-known herbs that are remarkably effective in combating stress.

The Top Calming Herbs

Holy Basil: Adaptogenic Powerhouse

Tulsi, or Holy basil as it is also called, is considered to be an adaptogen in Ayurvedic medicine, meaning that it can help the body modulate its reaction to stress.

- **Tea**: Boil the holy basil leaves to prepare a cup of tea, which will help in reducing stress.
- **Capsules**: For the maintenance of a healthy level of calmness throughout the day, one can take holy basil capsules.
- **Essential** Oil: You can include a few drops of holy basil essential oil into your diffuser for a fragrant, stress-busting companion.
- **Powder**: Holy basil powder can be easily blended into smoothies or juices to help manage stress.
- **Fresh Leaves**: A natural stress relief exercise is to chew fresh holy basil leaves every morning.

Rhodiola: The Energy Balancer

Rhodiola is an herb of the arctic regions of Europe and Asia, which has been used for centuries to promote the balance of energy and decrease stress.

- **Extract**: Rhodiola extract can be taken in the morning with a smoothie to start the day with balanced energy.
- **Capsules**: To help your body able to adapt to stress both physical and mental, then take rhodiola capsules.
- **Tea**: Use rhodiola root for a warming, balancing tea.
- **Tincture**: Rhodiola tincture can be taken by mixing it with water or any favorite juice, making it easy to take for stress.
- **Supplement Blend**: You may find Rhodiola in combination with other adaptogens in the supplement formulas meant for overall stress relief.

Ashwagandha: The Stress Regulator

Ashwagandha is a herb that has been used in Ayurvedic medicine for the treatment of stress and anxiety.

- **Powder**: Take ashwagandha powder in your morning coffee or mix it in your smoothies for a stress-relieving boost.
- **Capsules**: Ashwagandha capsules can be a convenient way to take as regards the use of this herb in our daily diet.
- **Tincture**: The tincture can be used in water or juice for quick absorption and stress relief.
- **Tea**: Use the root of ashwagandha to brew your relaxing evening tea.
- **Gummies**: Ashwagandha gummies are the best-recommended products that help to fight stress in a tasty way.

Creating a Calming Routine

Introducing these calming herbs into your diet can go a long way in improving your coping capacity with stress.

Morning Rituals: When you wake up and perform stress-reducing activities, it helps you to start the day on a positive note.

- **Herbal Tea**: The first drink in the morning should be a cup of tea prepared from holy basil leaves.
- **Essential Oil**: Apply holy basil essential oil in the shower in the morning to have a calming effect.
- **Capsules**: Rhodiola or ashwagandha capsules should be taken to maintain a level of calmness throughout the day.

- **Smoothie**: Add holy basil powder or take Rhodiola extract with your breakfast, or mix it with your morning smoothie.
- **Fresh Leaves**: Crush fresh holy basil and take it with some water in the morning as a way of starting your morning.

Midday Breaks: Taking time off during the day also has its advantages. For example, it can help reduce stress hence increasing productivity.

- **Herbal Snacks**: Include rhodiola-infused snacks like energy bars.
- **Tea Time**: Sip on some herbal tea in the middle of the day when you are having your lunch.
- **Breathing Exercises**: To increase the relaxing impact of your herbs, try incorporating deep breathing exercises that go hand in hand with the herbs.
- **Aromatherapy**: Put holy basil or ashwagandha essential oil in the diffuser at your workstation.
- **Supplement Blends**: Supplements that help to combat stress can be taken midday and should include Rhodiola and ashwagandha.

Evening Wind-Down: It is beneficial to take herbs that can help you relax before sleeping since they will enhance the quality of your sleep and the quality of your wakefulness.

- **Night Tea**: Holy basil or Rhodiola tea should be taken before going to bed.
- **Bath Soak**: You can also use ashwagandha essential oil in your bath water to help you relax.
- **Tincture**: Have a glass of holy basil tincture about an hour before you retire to bed to enable you to have a peaceful sleep.
- **Essential Oil**: Spray some calming essential oils in your bedroom.
- **Gummies**: Have ashwagandha gummies before sleep to help you calm down and have a good night's sleep.

Sleep Soundly

Sleep is one of the most important factors that determine the health of any person, but today, many people cannot get a good night's rest. Herbal teas and tinctures are also the best natural remedies for people who have sleeping disorders. This section gives details of some of the less usual herbs that may be useful in helping to get a good night's sleep.

Herbal Teas for Better Sleep

Skullcap

Skullcap is one of the most effective herbs when it comes to the nervous system, and as such, it is highly recommended for use in cases of sleeplessness.

- **Tea**: Skullcap leaves can be brewed to make a warm and calming drink before going to bed.
- **Tea Blend**: It is advised to blend skullcap with other herbs that have a sedative effect, such as lemon balm or passion flower.
- **Cold Brew**: Use skullcap tea to make a cold brew and add the taste to your drinks.
- **Powder**: Skullcap powder should be taken in the evening and mixed with the smoothie.
- **Capsules**: If you are not really up for preparing the tea, you can opt for skullcap capsules.

Blue Vervain

Blue Vervain is believed to have a soothing effect on the muscles of the body and, hence, is a good herb to help one to sleep.

- **Tea**: Steep dried blue vervain flowers in hot water for a relaxing tea.
- **Honey Blend**: Blue vervain can be taken as a tea mixed with honey to sweeten it and to help calm the nerves.
- **Herbal Mix**: Blue vervain can be used together with skullcap and hops to create a very effective sleep-inducing concoction.
- **Tincture**: Blue vervain tincture can be taken with water or juice so that it is absorbed into the body immediately.
- **Infused Oil**: Apply blue vervain oil in the evening before going to bed as you massage the body.

California Poppy

California poppy is usually taken together with other herbs for the improvement of the quality of sleep.

- **Tea**: Brew the California poppy along with other relaxing herbs such as skullcap and blue vervain.
- **Tea Bags**: It is recommended to purchase ready-made tea bags of California poppy for ease of use.
- **Blended Drinks**: Drink California poppy with your herbal teas in the evening for better relaxation.
- **Tincture**: Take California poppy tincture directly or in a beverage at night.
- **Capsules**: For the best results of using California poppy capsules, make it a habit to take them every night.

Tinctures for Restful Sleep

Herbal tinctures are potent liquid extracts that can be easily integrated into your night regime.

Skullcap Tincture: Skullcap tincture is quite concentrated and can be used for quick relief from insomnia.

- **Drops**: Take a few drops of skullcap tincture in water before going to sleep.
- **Sleep Blend**: If you are using skullcap tincture, then it should be used with other calming tinctures like blue vervain and California poppy.
- **Capsules**: For a convenient option, it is recommended to take the skullcap capsules before going to bed.
- **Tea Mix**: Mix skullcap tincture with your evening tea for enhanced results.
- **Beverage**: Skullcap tincture can be added to warm milk to make a mug of warm beverage perfect for nighttime consumption.

Blue Vervain Tincture: Blue vervain tincture is another effective remedy for improving the quality of sleep.

- **Mix**: Include blue vervain tincture in the herbal tea that you take in the evening.
- **Standalone**: Take a few drops sublingually, this helps in fast assimilation.
- **Combo**: It is used together with skullcap tincture for enhanced effects.
- **Water**: Dilute blue vervain tincture in a glass of water for a relaxing bedtime drink.
- **Juice**: Blue vervain tincture may be taken with fruit juice for a pleasant taste.

California Poppy Tincture: California poppy is also known to be an adaptogen that assists in restoring sleep as well as decreasing stress.

- **Evening Drink**: It can be consumed by adding California poppy tincture to warm tea or milk to be taken in the evening.
- **Relaxation Blend**: It can be blended with other soothing tinctures for an effective solution to sleep disorders.
- **Daily Use**: Regular use can help improve the general quality of sleep in the long run.
- **Direct Drops**: Place a few drops under the tongue for a quick result.
- **Smoothie**: Add some California poppy tincture to your nighttime smoothie for additional calming effects.

Chapter 3

Herbal Skincare

Y ou probably know that the skin is an organ, but did you know that it is the largest one in the body? This is why it must be nurtured and paid as much attention as any other part of the body. Herbal skincare is the use of natural products to treat your skin in a delicate manner as well as cure it.

Radiant Skin

Have you ever stood in front of the mirror and wished that you had naturally radiant skin? This is where herbal remedies provide a solution. Here is the list of botanicals that can change the future of skin health:

Cleansing with Herbal Infusions

The basic step to achieving glowing skin is through washing. The application of herbal infusions can help in the washing of the skin to get rid of dirt without affecting the skin's natural oils.

- **Chamomile**: Chamomile is also used for its anti-inflammatory effect; it is effective in soothing irritated skin and reducing redness. For example, brew chamomile and drink it with honey, or steep the chamomile and wash your face with it.
- **Lavender**: Lavender not only soothes the mind but also the skin, and therefore is a perfect addition to any wound dressing. It is particularly beneficial to skin with acne since it has antimicrobial activity. Mix a few drops of lavender oil into the soap that you use to wash your face.
- **Calendula**: This is one of the flowers that have healing and water-retaining properties, which are ideal for dry skin or skin with rashes. Prepare a tea by using dried calendula flowers and then apply it as a toner.
- **Green Tea**: Green tea is packed with antioxidants, and hence, it aids in preventing damaging effects on the skin due to environmental factors. Green tea bags used after they have been cooled can serve as a good compress.

Moisturizing with Herbal Oils

Drinking water is essential for the skin to be healthy and look radiant. The herbal oils can penetrate and enrich the skin with necessary substances and moisture.

- **Rosehip Oil**: Rich in vitamins A and C, rosehip oil aids in fading away scars and spots, making the skin lighter. Apply a few drops onto your face before you go to sleep at night.
- **Jojoba Oil**: Like the skin's own natural sebum, jojoba oil is suitable for all skin types. It hydrates without the clogging of pores. You can use it as a daily moisturizer.
- **Argan Oil**: Argan oil contains fatty acids that are useful for replenishing the elasticity and smoothness of the skin. Gently blend it with the everyday face cream that you prefer.
- **Sea Buckthorn Oil**: This vibrant orange oil contains antioxidants and omega fatty acids, which improve skin's texture and erase signs of aging. Use topically, or can be blended with other oils.

Herbal Face Masks

Facial masks work deep on the skin since they deliver a high concentration of active ingredients to the affected area. Herbal masks can cleanse, moisturize, and even tone up the skin of your face.

- **Turmeric and Honey Mask**: Turmeric is used to fight inflammation and honey to moisturize. This can help in eradicating pimples and lighten the skin. For this, a teaspoon of turmeric should be mixed with a tablespoon of honey and applied to the face for 10-15 minutes.
- **Oatmeal and Yogurt Mask**: Oatmeal has a soothing and exfoliating effect on the skin as yogurt helps in moisturizing and supplying probiotics. Mix oatmeal and yogurt in equal proportions, spread on the skin, and wash off with warm water after 15 minutes.
- **Aloe Vera and Cucumber Mask**: Aloe vera has healing and moisturizing properties, while cucumber cools and calms. Mix fresh aloe vera gel with cucumber slices and apply on the face.
- **Clay and Rose Water Mask**: Clay, for its part, acts as a cleanser to the skin, while rose water tightens and moisturizes the skin. Add one tablespoon of clay to rose water, make a paste, and apply the paste on the face.

Hair Care

Dreaming of having thick, shiny, and strong hair? Herbal treatments are an all-natural way to treat many hair problems. Now, let us look at some of the roles that plants have in hair care.

Herbal Rinses for Healthy Hair

Herbal rinses are beneficial in that they can improve the luster of hair, decrease dandruff, and improve the condition of the scalp. It is quite simple to prepare and can be integrated into the hair regimen.

- **Rosemary Rinse**: Aids in hair growth and increases blood flow to the area of the scalp where it is applied. Soak rosemary in water and boil it, let it cool, and use it as the last rinse after washing your hair with shampoo.
- **Nettle Rinse**: Nettle has tonic properties that are good for hair and prevent hair loss. Crush dried nettle leaves and steep them in boiling water, cool and rinse hair with it after washing.

- **Horsetail Rinse**: Horsetail is high in silica, and it assists in improving the strength of hair and reflects the shine. Use horsetail by boiling it in water and apply it as a final rinse.
- **Sage Rinse**: Sage is useful in that it aids in the process of making the hair darker where it begins to gray and also enhances the shine. Chop fresh or dry sage leaves and bring them to a boil in water, then cool and wash hair with it after washing with shampoo.

Herbal Oils for Hair Growth

It is also good to apply some of the herbal oils on the scalp and hair since they help nourish the roots, leading to reduced dandruff and an increase in hair growth.

- **Coconut Oil with Hibiscus**: The hibiscus flower is used in hair growth and to avoid early gray hair. Crush hibiscus petals and, mix with coconut oil and then massage the mixture on the scalp.
- **Olive Oil with Garlic**: Garlic nourishes the roots of the hair and helps in controlling the problem of hair fall. Add crushed garlic in olive oil and warm slightly before applying to the scalp.
- **Almond Oil with Amla**: Amla or Indian gooseberry is the best hair food as it contains vitamin C and antioxidants that help in hair regrowth and no dandruff. Crush a small amount of amla powder, add almond oil to it, and apply it to the hair.
- **Castor Oil with Fenugreek**: Fenugreek seeds are good for hair and help in hair regrowth and reduce hair fall. Soak fenugreek seeds in castor oil and apply the mixture to the head and hair.

Herbal Hair Masks

Hair masks give deep conditioning to the hair and are useful in combating certain hair problems like dryness, breakage, and others.

- **Avocado and Banana Mask**: Avocado moisturizes the hair, and bananas help to strengthen hair and make it shiny. Mash half an avocado and one banana together, apply it to the hair, and let it sit for 20 minutes.
- **Yogurt and Egg Mask**: Yogurt helps to restore the moisture and protein level of hair while egg helps to strengthen and give hair that shiny look. Beat one egg and add 1/2 cup of yogurt to it. Apply this mixture to the hair for 30 minutes.
- **Honey and Olive Oil Mask**: Honey is a moisturizing agent, while olive oil is a nutrient for the hair. Mix honey and olive oil in a 1:1 ratio; apply to the hair, and cover with a shower cap for 30 minutes.
- **Aloe Vera and Fenugreek Mask**: Aloe vera has anti-inflammatory properties that help the scalp, while fenugreek is good for hair strength. Mix aloe vera gel with freshly prepared fenugreek paste and massage the hair and scalp with it.

DIY Natural Herbal Beauty Cosmetics

Who needs commercial cosmetics when it is possible to make natural cosmetics at home? Cosmetics made from herbs and other natural products are safe and efficient and can be created according to the skin type of the client.

Herbal Lip Balms

Lip balms are products that are very crucial for the softening and moisturizing of the lips. Preparing your means that you are aware of what has been incorporated into your balm.

- **Beeswax and Coconut Oil Lip Balm**: Beeswax provides a protective barrier, and coconut oil helps moisturize the skin. To prepare this, melt 1 tablespoon of beeswax, 2 tablespoons of coconut oil, and a few drops of essential oil of your choice. Transfer to a small container and allow to cool.
- **Shea Butter and Lavender Lip Balm**: Shea butter is deeply moisturizing, and lavender oil is relaxing. To make the lotion, melt one tablespoon of shea butter with one teaspoon of coconut oil and a few drops of lavender oil. To use, melt over heat and then pour into the desired container.
- **Honey and Almond Oil Lip Balm**: Honey helps to soften the skin, while almond oil is beneficial for skin nutrition. To make the mixture, melt 1 teaspoon of honey, 1 tablespoon of almond oil, and 1 tablespoon of beeswax together. Stir until smooth and pour into the lip balm tubes.
- **Calendula and Olive Oil Lip Balm**: Calendula is known for treating chapped lips, while olive oil gives intensive conditioning. Squeeze calendula flowers with olive oil, filter, and add beeswax melted in water. Transfer into containers and cool.

Herbal Face Powders

Face powders are used to control oil and shine on the face and setting of makeup. Herbal face powders can be tinted to the skin type and give extra skincare benefits in addition to the tinting.

- **Arrowroot and Cocoa Powder**: Arrowroot powder absorbs excess oil from the skin, and cocoa powder gives a natural tone. To get the right color, blend one tablespoon of arrowroot powder with cocoa powder until you get the right color.
- **Cornstarch and Cinnamon**: Cornstarch also helps reduce oil, while cinnamon has antiseptic properties. To make a warm-toned powder, mix 2 tablespoons of cornstarch and 1/2 teaspoon of cinnamon.
- **Bentonite Clay and Nutmeg**: Bentonite clay helps in the detoxification of the skin while nutmeg imparts a natural sheen to the skin. To make the mask, mix 1 tablespoon of bentonite clay with a pinch of nutmeg.
- **Rice Flour and Beetroot Powder**: Rice flour makes the skin smooth, and beetroot powder gives the skin a rosy tint. Add 1 tablespoon of rice flour to beetroot powder to match your complexion.

Herbal Blush

Blush can make your cheeks look naturally rosy. Herbal blushes do not contain synthetic dyes and chemicals, instead of that, they use natural ingredients to give color.

- **Beetroot Powder Blush**: Beetroot powder is used for coloring and imparts a pretty pink color. Add beetroot powder to arrowroot powder to get a softer blush that can be easily blended in.
- **Hibiscus Powder Blush**: Hibiscus flowers are of very beautiful deep red color. Blend the hibiscus powder with cornstarch to get the preferred color.

- **Cocoa Powder and Cinnamon Blush**: To get a warm, bronzed look, mix cocoa powder with a small quantity of cinnamon and arrowroot powder.
- **Rose Petal Powder Blush**: Crush and pulverize rose petals until they become a powder-like substance. Blend it with a pinch of cornstarch to give a subtle, rosy blush.

Herbal Mascara

It is quite satisfying to make your mascara from scratch, as this will give you the best results. Herbal mascaras are mild to the eyes and can be made in different types and customized for length, volume, and color.

- **Activated Charcoal and Aloe Vera Gel Mascara**: Activated charcoal acts as a colorant while the aloe vera gel brings the aspect of a smooth feel. Combine 1 teaspoon of activated charcoal with 2 tablespoons of aloe vera gel.
- **Beeswax and Coconut Oil Mascara**: Beeswax is beneficial in increasing the thickness of the lashes while coconut oil moisturizes them. Mix 1 teaspoon of beeswax, 1 tablespoon of coconut oil and activated charcoal.
- **Black Tea and Shea Butter Mascara**: Black tea makes lashes darker and shea butter is for moisturizing. Brew black tea in hot water, then add melted shea butter and a little beeswax to it.
- **Cocoa Powder and Vitamin E Oil Mascara**: Cocoa powder gives a natural brown color, and vitamin E oil is good for the growth of the eyelashes. Mix 1 teaspoon of cocoa powder with 2 tablespoons of the aloe vera gel and a few drops of vitamin E oil.

Herbal Skin Ointments

Skin ointments can help many skin diseases, starting from dry skin to eczema. These homemade ointments tap into the restorative capacity of plants to nourish and protect the skin.

Healing Herbal Salves

Herbal salves are portable and can be used on injuries such as cuts, and scrapes as well as for dry skins. It is simple to prepare and very effective.

- **Calendula Salve**: Calendula is very effective in healing. Add calendula flowers to olive oil and boil it, then filter it, melt beeswax, and mix it. Transfer to the chosen containers and allow to cool.
- **Comfrey and Lavender Salve**: Comfrey has anti-inflammatory properties that will help in the regeneration of skin cells, while lavender is known to calm inflammation. Infuse comfrey and lavender in olive oil, strain, and combine with beeswax.
- **St. John's Wort and Coconut Oil Salve**: St. John's wort is very helpful in treating wounds, and coconut oil is very helpful in moisturizing the skin. Add St. John's wort to coconut oil and filter the mixture, then add beeswax to the mixture.
- **Plantain and Olive Oil Salve**: Plantain has functions of reducing inflammation and aiding in the healing of tissues. Infuse plantain leaves in olive oil, strain, and mix the solution with beeswax to get a plantain salve.

Soothing Eczema Balms

The management of eczema can be difficult but using herbal balms helps minimize the occurrences of flare-ups. This balm employs the use of natural products with a view of healing and providing comfort.

- **Chamomile and Shea Butter Balm**: Chamomile has anti-inflammatory properties, while shea butter is a moisturizer. Squeeze the chamomile and pour the liquid into olive oil. Add shea butter and beeswax.
- **Oatmeal and Coconut Oil Balm**: Oatmeal relieves the skin from inflammation, while coconut oil moisturizes the skin. Melt the coconut oil and beeswax and mix it with finely ground oatmeal.
- **Licorice Root and Aloe Vera Balm**: Licorice root has an anti-inflammatory effect, and aloe vera has a cooling effect on the skin. Infuse licorice root in olive oil, strain, and mix with aloe vera gel and beeswax.
- **Neem and Jojoba Oil Balm**: Neem is an effective fungicide and bactericide, while jojoba oil mimics the human skin's natural sebum. Infuse the neem leaves in jojoba oil, filter out the leaves, and add beeswax to the solution.

Anti-Aging Herbal Creams

Anti-aging creams can be used to minimize the formation of wrinkles and fine lines. Applying herbs has the benefit of providing the skin with the best treatment without the use of chemicals.

- **Rosehip and Aloe Vera Cream**: Rosehip oil contains vitamin A and vitamin C aids in minimizing the signs of aging. Blend the rosehip oil with aloe vera gel and beeswax to create a rejuvenating cream.
- **Green Tea and Shea Butter Cream**: Green tea is packed with antioxidants, while shea butter moisturizes deeply. Dissolve shea butter and beeswax, and add the brewed green tea to it after it has been cooled down.
- **Pomegranate and Coconut Oil Cream**: Pomegranate is believed to have anti-aging properties, while coconut oil is known to moisturize. Melt the coconut oil and beeswax and then mix it in with the pomegranate seed oil.
- **Lavender and Almond Oil Cream**: Lavender soothes the skin and erases fine lines, while almond oil gives the skin the nutrients it needs. Lavender essential oil added to almond oil and beeswax will help make a rich cream.

Herbal Sunscreens

Protect your skin from the sun. Herbal sunscreens are natural and don't contain chemicals that are found in commercial sunscreens.

- **Zinc Oxide and Coconut Oil Sunscreen**: Zinc oxide provides broad-spectrum protection, and coconut oil acts as a moisturizer. Combine zinc oxide with the melted coconut oil and beeswax.
- **Carrot Seed Oil and Shea Butter Sunscreen**: Carrot seed oil has natural UV protection, and shea butter will help moisturize the skin. Add carrot seed oil to shea butter and beeswax.
- **Raspberry Seed Oil and Aloe Vera Sunscreen**: Raspberry seed oil can protect the skin from the sun, while aloe vera has skin-healing properties. Mix raspberry seed oil with aloe vera gel and beeswax.

- **Green Tea and Jojoba Oil Sunscreen**: Green tea can protect the skin from UV radiation, and jojoba oil nourishes the skin. Mix steeped green tea with jojoba oil and beeswax.

Part II

Essential Oils

Aromatherapy for Well-being

Chapter 4

The Art and Science of Scent

Have you ever entered a room, and within five minutes of being in that room, you have become happy, sad, or relaxed just because of the smell? That is exactly the kind of magic aromas have. Smell is one of the most closely linked organs to human emotions and memory. This chapter focuses on the effects of essential oils and goes further into the details of their features and how to employ them properly.

Essential Oils and Their Properties

Essential oils are considered the lifeblood of plants. In other words, they are the liquids extracted from plants through the distillation process. These aromatic compounds have been used for many centuries to improve the quality of people's health. But what are these oils, and why are they so potent?

1. Lavender Oil

- **Stress Relief**: Lavender oil is said to have a calming effect on the nervous system. Sometimes, you just need to put a few drops in a diffuser and relax after a long day.
- **Sleep Aid**: Feeling sleepy at night and can't sleep? Aromatherapy has it that placing a lavender oil sachet under the pillow will help one have a sound sleep.
- **Skin Care**: lavender oil is quite useful in the treatment of minor burns and bites from insects due to its antiseptic nature.
- **Pain Relief**: Diluted lavender oil can be applied to areas of the body that are in pain, such as the muscles.
- **Hair Growth**: It may also be useful in improving the health of your scalp and stimulating hair growth.
- **Anti-Anxiety**: Lavender oil, when inhaled, has an impact on decreasing symptoms of anxiety and depression.

2. Peppermint Oil

- **Digestive Aid**: People have used peppermint oil for its effectiveness in alleviating gastrointestinal problems. A drop can be added to tea and taken for a refreshing remedy.
- **Headache Relief**: For tension headaches, a dab on the temples does the trick.
- **Respiratory Relief**: Inhaling peppermint oil is very helpful in clearing the sinus and, hence, improving breathing.

- **Energy Booster**: Its invigorating scent can enhance the alertness and energy of an individual.
- **Muscle Pain Relief**: It can be utilized for massage to alleviate muscle pain and decrease inflammation.
- **Insect Repellent**: Peppermint oil can repel ants, spiders, and any other small insects that may be in an area.

3. Tea Tree Oil

- **Acne Treatment**: Tea tree oil is one of the most effective remedies for acne since it has antibacterial properties.
- **Wound Care**: When you have cuts and scrapes, use diluted tea tree oil to avoid getting infected.
- **Anti-Fungal**: It's ideal for use in cases of fungal infections such as athlete's foot.
- **Dandruff Control**: It can help to minimize the occurrence of dandruff and, at the same time, make the scalp healthier.
- **Household Cleaner**: Tea tree oil can also be used as a natural disinfectant.
- **Mold Remover**: It can be used in fighting mold in moist areas such as the kitchen and the bathroom.

4. Eucalyptus Oil

- **Cold Relief**: Eucalyptus oil is used in many commercial cough and cold products that are available in the market. When inhaled, the vapor of this plant can help reduce congestion.
- **Muscle Pain**: It also has an anti-inflammatory effect that assists in the alleviation of muscle pain when incorporated in massage oils.
- **Insect Repellent**: Pests such as mosquitoes can be chased away by the use of Eucalyptus oil.
- **Immune Support**: It can be of help in enhancing the immune system and help to ward off infections.
- **Mental Clarity**: Its smell is quite invigorating, and it can help to enhance concentration and productivity.
- **Wound Healing**: Eucalyptus oil has properties that can help in the treatment of minor injuries such as cuts and abrasions.

5. Lemon Oil

- **Mood Booster**: Lemon oil is traditionally associated with freshness and cleanliness; its smell can have a positive effect on a person's mood.
- **Natural Cleaner**: It is a great natural cleaner that can be used to clean surfaces and remove germs.
- **Skin Brightener**: Essential lemon oil can help in skin lightening, and thus it can be included in skincare products.
- **Detoxification**: It can help to detoxify the body when taken in moderation.
- **Insect Repellent**: Lemon oil is effective against mosquitoes and fleas, as it has insect-repellant properties.
- **Air Freshener**: It can be used to freshen and purify indoor air.

6. Rosemary Oil

- **Cognitive Boost**: It is said that the use of rosemary oil helps in boosting memory and concentration faculties.
- **Hair Growth**: It helps to activate hair follicles and makes your hair grow healthy.
- **Pain Relief**: Due to its anti-inflammatory properties, it can be used to treat muscle and joint pains.
- **Immune Support**: In addition, Rosemary oil can increase the immunity of the body.
- **Stress Reduction**: It can help in relieving stress and anxiety when inhaled.
- **Digestive Health**: It is also known that rosemary oil helps to improve digestion and to relieve stomach cramps.

The Science Behind Essential Oils

These oils have different components, such as terpenes, esters, and aldehydes, and each of the components contributes to the characteristics of the oil. An understanding of these components aids in the optimization of the oils' functionalities.

- **Terpenes**: As found in many essential oils, terpenes are anti-inflammatory, antiviral, and antibacterial.
- **Esters**: Used for their calming effects, esters are present in oils such as lavender and bergamot.
- **Aldehydes**: These compounds which are present in oils like lemongrass, possess severe anti-inflammatory and sedative properties.
- **Ketones**: Existing in oils such as rosemary, ketones are instrumental in the regeneration of tissues and the support of the mucous membrane.
- **Phenols**: A type of antioxidant that can be identified in oils such as thyme, phenols possess antimicrobial and immune-enhancing capabilities.

Safe and Effective Use of Essential Oils

Some oils are very helpful, but they should never be taken internally without consulting a professional. Side effects can occur if misused, so it is important to know how to use them properly.

1. Dilution

Essential oils are very potent and should not be used directly on the skin. Adding them to carrier oils such as coconut or Jojoba oil is crucial to avoid skin reactions in the users.

- **General Rule**: The dilution ratio should be safe for use and normally ranges between 2-3 drops of the essential oil per teaspoon of the carrier oil.
- **Sensitive Areas**: Do not apply the essential oils on the face, especially around the eyes, ears, mouth, or any other mucous membranes.
- **Patch Test**: It is always advisable to do a patch test any time you are introducing a new essential oil. Rub a small amount of the diluted oil on your forearm and allow it to dry before washing your hands; wait for 24 hours to see if there is any irritation.

- **Children and Pets**: Some individuals, such as children and pets, are more sensitive to essential oils, and therefore, one should use lower dilution ratios for them.
- **Pregnancy**: Some oils should not be taken during pregnancy. Do not take any action without the advice of a healthcare professional.
- **Elderly**: They also need lower dilution ratios because the skin of older people is more sensitive as compared to younger individuals.

2. Proper Inhalation Techniques

Inhalation is one of the most effective methods of use of essential oils. However, there are safe ways through which one can go about to get the best out of aromatherapy sessions.

- **Diffusers**: Disperse the oil in the air through the use of a diffuser. It is recommended to use the correct proportion of oil and water as recommended by the manufacturer.
- **Steam Inhalation**: Place a couple of drops of the essential oil in a bowl of hot water. Cover yourself with a towel, lean over the bowl of hot water, and breathe in the steam for about 5-10 minutes.
- **Direct Inhalation**: To have a quick boost, take a whiff straight from the bottle or put a drop on your hands and bring it to your nose.
- **Inhalers**: Personal inhalers can be used for targeted relief and convenience.
- **Aromatherapy Jewelry**: Diffuser necklaces and bracelets help you to carry the benefits of the essential oils with you.

3. Topical Application

Topical application can be used in cases where the affected area is known such as the case of muscle pains or skin diseases. However, knowing where and how to use the oils is very important.

- **Massage**: The diluted essential oils may be applied in massages to help relax the tight muscles and increase blood circulation. Concentrate on areas of tension such as the neck, shoulders, and back.
- **Skincare**: For acne or other skin problems, you can use a cotton ball to apply the diluted oil on the affected part of the skin. It is always recommended to use oils appropriate for your skin type.
- **Compresses**: In this case, you can wet a cloth with water and a few drops of essential oil and apply the wet cloth on the affected muscles or joints.
- **Reflexology**: Massage oils are used on certain areas of the feet or hands for targeted relief.
- **Baths**: Mix diluted oils with your bath water for a relaxing experience.
- **Lotions and Creams**: Include the oils in your choice of lotions and creams for better results.

4. Internal Use

While some types of essential oils are safe to be ingested, this practice is highly debatable and should be done with caution. It is always recommended to seek the advice of a doctor before using any essential oils.

- **Quality Matters**: Always ensure you have high-quality, therapeutic-grade oils for internal consumption.
- **Dosage**: Follow the recommended dosage, and it should be strictly adhered to to prevent toxicity.
- **Consultation**: It is recommended that one consult an aromatherapist or a healthcare practitioner before taking any internally.
- **Dilution**: Oils should be taken with dilution when taken internally to prevent irritation.
- **Capsules**: Vegetable capsules should be used to take oils since they are harmless.
- **Mix with Food**: Incorporate oils into your meals for a safe way to consume them.

5. Storing Essential Oils

Storing of the oils should be done appropriately to retain the efficacy of the oils.

- **Dark Glass Bottles**: Light and UV rays have a deleterious effect on oils; therefore, store oils in dark glass bottles.
- **Cool, Dark Place**: Store your oils in a cool and dark area to avoid oxidation and degrading of the oil.
- **Tightly Sealed**: Make sure the bottles are properly closed to minimize the amount of evaporation and other external influences.
- **Avoid Heat**: It should also be noted that oils should not be stored in areas where there is direct exposure to sources of heat.
- **Check Expiry Dates**: To ensure the effectiveness, track the expiration dates.
- **Original Containers**: To prevent cross-contamination, store oils in their respective containers in which they were bought.

Chapter 5

Essential Oils for Physical Health

Have you ever got that feeling of relief from just a mere natural cure? Essential oils do that and much more, providing people with all the accumulated knowledge of the ages brought to the contemporary practice of health improvement. These extracts are not only for the smell; they are the solutions to some of the physical sicknesses you never thought could be cured naturally. Dive right in to find out how you can change the way you look at health through essential oils.

Pain Relief

Pain, many times, can be described as a constant companion – a shadow that one cannot seem to shake off. Fortunately, essential oils are a safe remedy for the common ailments that people usually take medicines for. These aromatic allies can alleviate pain and help with your mission to live a life free of pain.

The Magic of Essential Oils for Pain Relief

Oil extracts have been in existence for centuries and have been used to treat muscle and joint pains. From pains that may be experienced after exercising, to joint pains due to arthritis, these plant extracts can help in managing the pains without having to use drugs. Here are some of the most effective essential oils for pain relief:

- **Frankincense Oil**: It is known to have anti-inflammatory benefits and, thus, can effectively be used to reduce swelling and enhance blood flow.
- **Marjoram Oil**: It is used for muscle relaxation and relieving joint pains and is essential for people with arthritis.
- **Helichrysum Oil**: This oil is very effective for the treatment of bruises as well as muscle pains because of its strong anti-inflammatory and analgesic qualities.
- **Wintergreen Oil**: It has methyl salicylate which works like an aspirin, thus useful in managing headaches and muscle aches.

How to Use Essential Oils for Pain Relief

Some of the ways one can use essential oils for pain relief are by directly applying the oil on the affected part or using the oil in a warm bath. Here are some methods to try:

- **Topical Application**: Mix it with a base oil such as almond or avocado oil and apply topically to the skin.
- **Aromatherapy**: Breathe in essential oils that relieve pain and stress by using a diffuser.
- **Compress**: Take a basin of warm water and add a few drops of the essential oil, soak a cloth into it, then place the cloth on the affected area for about half an hour.

Recipes for Pain Relief

Blending oil by oneself can be a fun and effective way of handling pain. Here are a few recipes to try:

- **Muscle Relaxant**: In a 2-tablespoon carrier oil, dilute 5 drops of frankincense oil, 4 drops of marjoram oil, and 3 drops of helichrysum oil. Massage into sore muscles.
- **Arthritis Relief**: In a 2-tablespoon carrier oil, mix 6 drops of marjoram oil, 5 drops of wintergreen oil, and 4 drops of helichrysum oil. Apply to aching joints.
- **Post-Workout Soak**: To warm water, add 7 drops of frankincense oil, 6 drops of wintergreen oil, and 5 drops of helichrysum oil.

Precautions

While essential oils are generally safe, it's important to use them properly to avoid adverse reactions:

- **Dilution**: Do not use the essential oils raw on the skin; it is good to mix them with a carrier oil.
- **Patch Test**: It is also recommended that one should do a patch test on a small area of skin to see if the person has an allergy to the product.
- **Consult a Professional**: People with chronic illnesses or pregnant women should seek the services of a doctor before using oils.

Respiratory Support

Respiratory problems can be as simple as mild inconvenience to a severe problem that can be life-threatening. Aromatherapy from essential oils helps to unblock the airways and breathe easier. Learn how the power of these plants can make your breathing a lot more comfortable and effortless.

Essential Oils for Respiratory Health

In the context of respiratory support, oils are some of the most beneficial you can use. They can aid in unblocking the airways, decrease inflammation, and also assist in the fight against infections. Here are some top essential oils for respiratory health:

- **Niaouli Oil**: Popular for its effectiveness in unblocking the nostrils and boosting the respiratory system.
- **Hyssop Oil**: This oil is useful in reducing the secretion of mucus and successfully treating cases of bronchitis and asthma.
- **Pine Needle Oil**: Due to its antiseptic nature, it can be employed to cure respiratory infections and to help remove congestion.
- **Cardamom Oil**: Has a warming sensation which is quite helpful when it comes to clearing the respiratory tracts and managing breathing issues.

Methods to Use Essential Oils for Respiratory Support

Incorporating essential oils into your routine for respiratory support can be done in several ways:

- **Steam Inhalation**: The best way to do this is to put a few drops of the essential oil in a bowl of hot water. Use a towel to cover your head over the water and breathe in the steam.
- **Diffusion**: Employ a diffuser to spread the oil in the air for easy breathing since this will help in the absorption of the fragrance.
- **Chest Rub**: To use essential oils, dilute them with a carrier oil and massage on the chest to ease breathing and congestion.

Recipes for Respiratory Support

Here are some effective essential oil blends to support respiratory health:

- **Congestion Buster**: In 2 tablespoons carrier oil, add 5 drops of niaouli oil, 4 drops of hyssop oil, and 4 drops of pine needle oil. Rub on the chest and back.
- **Sinus Relief**: Mix Hyssop oil 4 drops, pine needle oil 3 drops, cardamom oil 3 drops, carrier oil 1 teaspoon. Apply to temples and neck.
- **Easy Breathing Blend**: To prepare the mixture for the skin, one has to mix 6 drops of niaouli oil, 5 drops of cardamom oil, and 4 drops of pine needle oil with 2 tablespoons of carrier oil. Rub onto the chest and then take a deep breath.

Tips for Using Essential Oils Safely

To maximize the benefits of essential oils for respiratory support, follow these safety tips:

- **Proper Dilution**: Make sure that the essential oils are well diluted with the carrier oils so as not to cause skin reactions on the skin.
- **Avoid Ingestion**: Some of the essential oils should not be ingested without the recommendation of a doctor.
- **Sensitive Individuals**: For those who have asthma and other respiratory conditions, it is advisable to seek advice from a medical practitioner regarding the use of essential oils.

Digestive Harmony

Gastrointestinal problems are known to affect the overall quality of an individual's life due to physical discomfort and inconvenience. Digestive system oils are also useful in the management of digestive system imbalances by maintaining intestinal health. Now, let's look at the ways aromatherapy can help you to balance your digestion.

Essential Oils for Digestive Health

The digestive benefits of essential oils have been known for ages, and they are also used to relieve the gastrointestinal tract. The potent plant extracts present in it can aid in the healing of the digestive tract, decrease inflammation, and improve digestion. Here are some of the most effective essential oils for digestive harmony:

- **Ginger Oil**: Ginger oil is useful for combating inflammation and flatulence, and it may alleviate the feeling of bloating and nausea.
- **Peppermint Oil**: Peppermint oil contains menthol that relieves the muscle of the gastrointestinal tract, hence, useful in treating IBS and indigestion.
- **Fennel Oil**: Fennel oil can help in digestion since it encourages the production of enzymes that facilitate digestion, and reduces cases of bloated stomachs and gas production.
- **Chamomile Oil**: Chamomile oil is known to have a relaxing effect, which makes it useful in easing an upset stomach and decreasing cramps and spasms.

Methods to Use Essential Oils for Digestive Support

It is easy to use essential oils for digestive health, and here are some ways that will help you:

- **Topical Application**: Mix the essential oils with a carrier oil and rub on the abdomen in circles, starting from the right side and going clockwise to aid digestion.
- **Aromatherapy**: Inhale the vapors of essential oils by using a diffuser, as it can help in easing the nerves in the stomach.
- **Internal Use**: Though some oils are safe to be taken internally, they should only be taken in modest amounts and under the supervision of a physician.

Recipes for Digestive Harmony

It can be fun to come up with essential oils for digestive health since it is a creative way of promoting good digestion. Here are a few recipes to try:

- **Bloating Relief**: Take 5 drops of ginger oil, 5 drops of fennel oil, and 5 drops of peppermint oil and add them to 2 tablespoons of carrier oil. Rub on the abdomen to ease the feeling of bloating and gas.
- **Nausea Ease**: Mix 3 drops of peppermint oil, 3 drops of chamomile oil, and 3 drops of ginger oil with one teaspoon of carrier oil. Apply to the temples and wrists for the nausea.
- **Digestive Aid**: Mix 4 drops of fennel oil, 4 drops of ginger oil, and 4 drops of peppermint oil with 2 tablespoons of carrier oil. Rub over the abdomen in circular motions to help in digestion.

Tips for Using Essential Oils Safely

To maximize the benefits of essential oils for digestive support, follow these safety tips:

- **Proper Dilution**: It is recommended that essential oils are diluted with a carrier oil to avoid skin irritation.
- **Patch Test**: Before applying it on the body, one should apply it on a small area of the skin to determine if it causes any reaction.
- **Consult a Professional**: Some of the essential oils may hurt your digestive system, especially if you are suffering from a chronic digestive ailment or if you are pregnant. Therefore, it is advised to consult a doctor before using essential oils.

Essential Oils for Exercise and Workouts

It is important to engage in physical activities to enhance the body's well-being; however, this can also cause muscle pain and fatigue. The use of essential oils can benefit your workout session by increasing energy, performance, and recovery time. See how these natural treatments help in your fitness plans.

Essential Oils for Pre-Workout Energy Boost

The morale and energy levels in the morning are very important when it comes to exercising and exercising properly. Here are some essential oils that can help energize and prepare your body for exercise:

- **Lemon Oil**: Lemon oil has a very uplifting and energizing effect; thus, it can be used to improve energy and focus.
- **Eucalyptus Oil**: Eucalyptus oil is good for the respiratory system, and this makes it easier for you to breathe during cardio workouts.
- **Peppermint Oil**: The scent of peppermint oil can improve focus and reduce the level of drowsiness.
- **Grapefruit Oil**: Grapefruit oil is known to help in increasing metabolic rate and energy levels; hence can be used before working out.

Methods to Use Essential Oils for Pre-Workout

Incorporating essential oils in your pre-workout regimen can help you maximize your performance. Here are some methods to try:

- **Aromatherapy**: Essential oils can be inhaled using a diffuser before the workout.
- **Topical Application**: Mix with carrier oil and rub on the wrists or on the chest to breathe in the aroma while exercising.
- **Inhalation**: You can use essential oil by putting a few drops on a cotton wool or tissue and smelling it before going to the gym.

Essential Oils for Post-Workout Recovery

Recovery is as important as the actual exercising. Essential oils assist in relieving muscle pain, inflammation, and relaxation. Here are some essential oils that are beneficial for post-workout recovery:

- **Lavender Oil**: This oil is famous for its calming and anti-inflammatory effects, which can be used to massage the sore muscles and make the organism relax.
- **Marjoram Oil**: Marjoram oil is useful in relaxing muscles and in the treatment of spasms and cramps.
- **Rosemary Oil**: This oil is useful in increasing blood flow and in alleviating pains and aches in muscles.
- **Clary Sage Oil**: Clary sage oil can also be useful in decreasing inflammation as well as helping one relax after exercise.

Methods to Use Essential Oils for Post-Workout Recovery

Using oils after a workout session will help the body to recover in the shortest time possible. Here are some methods to try:

- **Massage**: Mix essential oils with carrier oil and rub on the affected area to cure muscle pain and inflammation.
- **Bath Soak**: This can be done by putting a few drops of the essential oil in warm water to have a warm bath to soothe the muscles.
- **Compress**: In a basin of warm water, mix some drops of essential oils and soak a cloth in it, then apply on the sore muscles for about 15-20 minutes.

Recipes for Post-Workout Recovery

It can be quite enjoyable to prepare your blends of oils to help with the body's recovery after a workout session. Here are a few recipes to try:

- **Muscle Relief**: Lavender oil, marjoram oil, and rosemary oil – 5 drops each; Carrier oil – 2 tablespoons. Massage onto sore muscles.
- **Relaxation Bath**: It is recommended that 7 drops of clary sage oil, 6 drops of lavender oil, and 5 drops of marjoram oil should be mixed in a warm bath.
- **Pain Relief Compress**: Take 4 drops of rosemary oil, 4 drops of clary sage oil, and 4 drops of lavender oil and mix with warm water. Take the mixture and dip a cloth in it, then rub the cloth on the affected muscles.

Tips for Using Essential Oils Safely

To maximize the benefits of essential oils for exercise and workouts, follow these safety tips:

- **Proper Dilution**: It is also important to make sure that essential oils are adequately mixed with carrier oil so as not to cause skin irritation.
- **Patch Test**: One should do a patch test on the skin to check for any allergic reaction.
- **Consult a Professional**: Do not use essential oils if you have any chronic illness or if you are pregnant; first, seek advice from your doctor.

Chapter 6

Essential Oils for Emotional Balance

Healing and finding happiness is never easy, but with the help of essential oils, it is possible to achieve a state of balance and wholeness. These natural plant extracts have been in use for centuries for their ability to soothe the mind and the spirit. When you use essential oils, there is a way you can make your life a haven of positivity; here are some tips. The nature of the oils is that they can influence certain emotions like stress, joy, and love. Let's understand how these natural remedies can impact your emotional well-being.

Stress Management

The stress of life can become too much at some point, and you will be looking for a moment of stillness and normalcy. Stress can be managed using essential oils since they provide a calming impact on the body. Thus, you can choose the necessary oils to create a calm atmosphere and navigate challenges with ease.

Stress Relief with Essential Oils

- **Natural Calming Agents**: Some of the oils that are used when seeking to induce relaxation are lavender, chamomile, sandalwood, frankincense, and vetiver.
  - **Lavender**: It is used for relaxation due to its sweet, floral aroma, which alleviates anxiety. Lavender oil, when inhaled, helps to soothe the nervous system and decrease stress.
  - **Chamomile**: Chamomile oil is also used in teas and has a relaxing impact on the body and mind. It is especially useful in the treatment of stress and anxiety-related symptoms.
  - **Sandalwood**: This oil is renowned for its excellent grounding properties, which means that it helps to stabilize emotions and find inner harmony. Being in a position to make the right decisions can make you feel more in control and stable.
  - **Frankincense**: Frankincense oil is used in spirituality and meditation to reduce the rate of breathing and bring about relaxation. It is ideal for meditation and other similar practices.
  - **Vetiver**: Commonly known as the "oil of tranquility," vetiver is one of the most grounding oils and perfect for those who are feeling a bit lost or stressed. It can prove useful in calming the frayed nerves.

Creating Calming Blends

- **Lavender and Chamomile Blend**

- o **Benefits**: This combination is perfect for nighttime when you want to relax and prepare for sleep. It enhances sleep quality and helps to overcome such disorders as anxiety at night.
  - o **Usage**: Try putting a couple of drops of each oil in a diffuser in your bedroom or dilute them with a carrier oil for a gentle skin massage.
- **Sandalwood and Frankincense Blend**
  - o **Benefits**: This is one of the best blends to use when you want to meditate or calm yourself and create a serene atmosphere.
  - o **Usage**: During yoga or meditation, add some drops in a diffuser or apply to the skin and rub on the wrists and other pulse points.
- **Vetiver and Lavender Blend**
  - o **Benefits**: This blend is one of the best for combating stress throughout the day. It gives a soothing feeling without any soporific effect on the body.
  - o **Usage**: Inhale directly from the bottle or put some drops into a handkerchief to have it with you at any time.

Application Techniques

- **Aromatherapy**
  - o **Diffusers**: Diffusers can be employed to spread the calming blends in the house or working place to foster a relaxing atmosphere.
  - o **Inhalation**: Take a whiff straight from the bottle or from a couple of drops on a tissue for instant tension release.
- **Topical Application**
  - o **Massage**: Mix the essential oils with a carrier oil and then apply the mixture to the skin to reduce tension and achieve relaxation.
  - o **Bath Soaks**: Add a few drops of essential oils to a warm bath to relax the body and the mind from stress.

Safety Precautions

- **Dilution**: Always mix essential oils with a carrier oil before applying to the skin to avoid irritation.
  - o **Proper Ratios**: Usually, a 2-3% dilution level (12-18 drops of essential oil per ounce of carrier oil) is safe for most adults.
- **Patch Test**: Carry out a patch test to determine whether there will be any reactions in the skin.
  - o **Method**: Take a drop of oil and mix it with a large amount of water, then rub it on one's skin and wait for 24 hours to see if there is any redness or itching.
- **Consult a Professional**: If one has a medical condition or is pregnant, he/she should consult a doctor before using essential oils.

Personal Experience

Cognitive researchers have realized that a lot of people have benefited from the use of essential oils when it comes to stress. Real-life experiences tend to focus on the transformative nature of these natural remedies in one's life. For instance, people working in stressful occupations claim that using essential oils makes them feel more stable and less stressed.

Mood Enhancement

It is also imperative to note that happiness is significant in life and this is why essential oils can be so useful in the enhancement of your moods. These natural extracts not only give you a good feeling through your taste buds but also have an impact on your well-being. Essential oils, therefore, make it possible for you to find inspiration and give you a positive outlook on life daily.

How Essential Oils Enhance Mood

- **Natural Mood Boosters**: Some of the oils that are believed to have uplifting properties include citrus oils, rosemary, jasmine, bergamot, and ylang-ylang.
  - **Citrus Oils**: Oils that are stimulating include lemon oil, orange oil, and grapefruit oil, as they are known to give one positive energy. They have crisp, invigorating smells that help the senses and create the feeling of happiness and energy.
  - **Rosemary**: It is an herbaceous oil that not only works wonders for memory and concentration but also combats mental fatigue and lifts moods.
  - **Jasmine**: Jasmine oil has a sweet, exotic smell and is regarded as a remarkable mood booster that helps to get rid of the states of pessimism and apathy.
  - **Bergamot**: This oil has a pleasant, fresh, and citrus-like smell that will help lessen depression and anxiety to make you happy.
  - **Ylang-Ylang**: Ylang-ylang oil is another oil with a sweet and floral scent that aids in decreasing stress levels and improving moods for relaxation and balance.

Creating Uplifting Blends

- **Citrus and Rosemary Blend**
  - **Benefits**: In its composition, this blend is invigorating and perfect for the morning schedule. It assists in waking and getting ready for the day.
  - **Usage**: Use it in a diffuser during the morning or dilute it with a carrier oil for a rejuvenating body oil.
- **Jasmine and Bergamot Blend**
  - **Benefits**: Perfect for use in lifting morale and creating a feeling of happiness. This blend is ideal for use when one needs to be cheered up.
  - **Usage**: Diffuse in living areas or mix with a carrier oil and apply to areas of the body that have a pulse for constant uplifting of mood.
- **Ylang-Ylang and Citrus Blend**
  - **Benefits**: This combination is effective in relieving stress and in raising mood at the same time.

o **Usage**: Spray into a diffuser or add a few drops into the warm bath for the best aromatherapy experience.

Application Techniques

- **Aromatherapy**
  - **Diffusers**: Incorporate aromatherapy diffusers to emit positive fragrances in the environment you spend most of your time in or at your workplace.
  - **Inhalation**: Breathe directly from the bottle or several drops put on a piece of cloth for an immediate mood boost.
- **Topical Application**
  - **Massage**: Mix the essential oils with a carrier oil and apply on the skin to help in uplifting the mood as well as in reducing stress.
  - **Body Sprays**: Prepare a body spray by putting a few drops of essential oil in water and a few drops of witch hazel in a spray bottle. Use it throughout the day to uplift your mood.
- **Environmental Use**
  - **Room Sprays**: Dilute the essential oils in water and spray them around your house to create a cheerful atmosphere.
  - **Scented Candles**: Place a few drops of essential oils in containers of unscented candles to spread positive scents across the rooms.

Safety Precautions

- **Dilution**: It is recommended that essential oils should be mixed with carrier oil before applying on the skin to avoid skin reactions.
  - **Proper Ratios**: Generally, a 2-3% dilution is safe for most people, and this will require approximately 12-18 drops of essential oil per 1 ounce of the carrier oil.
- **Patch Test**: Do a patch test to check if there will be any allergic reactions.
  - **Method**: Dip a cotton ball in diluted oil, rub it on the skin, and then leave it for a whole day to see if there will be any reaction.
- **Consult a Professional**: It is also important to consult a doctor before using essential oils if you have certain illnesses or are pregnant.

Personal Experience

Many people have described the benefits of using essential oils and how they have helped with their state of mind and emotions. Tales of happiness and triumph over emotional obstacles using the help of these natural remedies are not rare. For instance, people suffering from seasonal affective disorder (SAD) have benefited from citrus oils in their day-to-day lives.

Sleep Improvement

Sleep is a vital part of human life, and a good night's sleep is crucial for good health. However, it is sad to note that many people suffer from insomnia or have poor sleep quality, which, in one way or another, impacts their lives. Of the many benefits of using essential oils, one of them is enhancing the quality of sleep. These aromatic extracts can also make an environment serene and enable the body, as well as the mind, to rest, which will make it easier for one to sleep.

The Role of Essential Oils in Sleep Improvement

- **Natural Sleep Aids**: Essential oils such as lavender, chamomile, cedarwood, sandalwood, and bergamot are some of the oils that are said to promote sleep.
  - o **Lavender**: This is a very useful oil that has many applications, mainly due to its ability to induce calmness and sedative effects. Research indicated that lavender can improve sleep quality by reducing anxiety and promoting relaxation.
  - o **Chamomile**: Chamomile often consumed as tea, has mild sedative properties that are beneficial when it comes to helping the mind and body relax before going to sleep.
  - o **Cedarwood**: This oil has a warm, woody undertone that is somewhat reminiscent of cedar and is perfect for use at night.
  - o **Sandalwood**: Sandalwood has a warm, earthy scent, and is used to calm the mind and the muscles, which will help one to sleep better.
  - o **Bergamot**: Unlike other oils, bergamot is not stimulating. Rather, it has more of a soothing influence that contributes to the diminishing of stress and anxiety, which then leads to a good night's sleep.

Creating Sleep-Enhancing Blends

- **Lavender and Chamomile Blend**
  - o **Benefits**: This combination is ideal for setting up a good night's sleep. It also assists in the reduction of stress and contributes to relaxation, thus enabling you to sleep well.
  - o **Usage**: Add a couple of drops of each oil in a diffuser in your bedroom or dilute with a carrier oil for a relaxing massage at night.
- **Cedarwood and Sandalwood Blend**
  - o **Benefits**: This combination gives the place a warm and relaxing environment, suitable for relaxation after work.
  - o **Usage**: An excellent way is to put it into a diffuser or mix it with water and apply the solution to the soles of your feet and the pulse points.
- **Bergamot and Lavender Blend**

  - o **Benefits**: This combination assists in lowering stress and anxiety levels and thus enables the person to have a good, uninterrupted sleep.
  - o **Usage**: Spray in the evening or even put a few drops on your pillow or the blanket.

Application Techniques

- **Aromatherapy**

- o **Diffusers**: One of the most efficient ways to set up an atmosphere favorable for sleep is to use a diffuser for spreading essential oils in the air. Place an aroma diffuser in the bedroom and switch it on at least half an hour before you go to bed.
  - o **Inhalation**: Inhale oils from the bottle or a few drops placed on a tissue for immediate relief.
- **Topical Application**
  - o **Massage**: Mix essential oils with a carrier oil and apply on the skin to help soothe the body and prepare for sleep. Concentrate on such zones as the neck, shoulders, and feet since people usually have a lot of tension there.
  - o **Bath Soaks**: Some essential oils can be added to a warm bathtub. This is very effective in relaxing muscles and the mind as well. This is a good way of creating a signal for your body in preparation for sleeping time.
  - o **Pillow Sprays**: To make a pillow spray, you can add several drops of the essential oil in a spray bottle with water and a little bit of witch hazel. Mist your pillow and the sheets before going to bed to ensure you have a good-smelling scent for the night.

Safety Precautions

- **Dilution**: When using essential oils, it is advisable to mix them with carrier oil before applying them on the skin, as this may cause skin irritation.
  - o **Proper Ratios**: Most commonly, 2-3% dilution or 12-18 drops of essential oil per ounce of the carrier oil is considered safe for an adult.
- **Patch Test**: Before application, do a patch test to determine whether there will be any allergic reactions.
  - o **Method**: Rub a small quantity of the diluted oil on a small area of the skin and observe the area after one whole day.
- **Consult a Professional**: If you have any chronic diseases or are pregnant, consult your doctor before using essential oils.
  - o **Pregnancy and Children**: Some oils need to be avoided when pregnant or when used for children; hence, one has to be careful or seek advice from a professional.

Part II

Food as Medicine

Chapter 7

The Healing Power of Food

There exists a close relation between food and mood. Food is not just a necessity; it is a therapeutic agent that helps in the recovery process. Thus, by selecting proper food, we are capable of improving our health, increasing our immunity, and avoiding numerous illnesses and chronic diseases. When you learn the benefits of food for the body, you can start a process of getting healthy, starting with the next meal that you are going to take. Now, let's discover how you can use the new understanding of the role of food as a medicine to support your health and well-being.

Nutrient-Dense Foods for Optimal Health

Good health is, therefore, a product of eating healthy foods that provide the body with the nutrients it requires. These foods are rich in vitamins and minerals and contain antioxidants that are necessary for effective body functioning. The fact is that by incorporating nutrient-rich foods into your daily meal plan, you are creating a solid ground that will lead you to a healthier and happier life.

Nutrient Density

Nutrient-dense foods are those foods that contain a large amount of vitamins, minerals, and other nutrients as compared to the energy they provide in the form of calories.

- **Benefits**: These foods have a higher density as they are rich in nutrients per calorie, thus are effective in boosting health without much calorie intake. It is especially useful for those who want to control their weight but at the same time receive all the necessary nutrients.
- **Examples**: Some familiar examples of such foods are green vegetables, berries, nuts, and seeds. Most of these foods are easily accessible and can be easily included in different meals and snacks.

Key Nutrient-Dense Foods

- **Leafy Greens**
    - **Nutritional Profile**: Kale, spinach, and Swiss chard contain vitamins A, C, and K, folates, and iron.
    - **Health Benefits**: These greens are beneficial to the immune system and bones, and they help to lower inflammation. They are also rich in fiber and thus play a big role in facilitating proper digestion and good flora in the gut.
- **Berries**
    - **Nutritional Profile**: Blueberries, strawberries, and raspberries contain vitamins C and K, fibers, and antioxidants.

- o **Health Benefits**: By consuming berries, one is protected from oxidative stress, inflammation, and heart diseases. They also have benefits like enhancing the health of the brain and also assist in weight loss, making them a perfect addition to your diet.
- o **Nuts and Seeds**
  - o **Nutritional Profile**: In almonds, chia seeds, and flax seeds are healthy fats, proteins, dietary fiber, and essential minerals, including magnesium and zinc.
  - o **Health Benefits**: They are beneficial for the heart, regulate the blood sugar levels, and ensure that one gets a sustained energy level. They are also good for skin health and weight control, as they provide a good snack that is healthy and can help one avoid unhealthy snacks.
- o **Whole Grains**
  - o **Nutritional Profile**: Quinoa, brown rice, and oatmeal are some of the best sources of fiber, B vitamins, and minerals such as iron and magnesium.
  - o **Health Benefits**: It is a known fact that whole grains enhance the digestive system, promote heart health, and regulate blood sugar levels. They also offer sustained energy and, therefore, form a good source of nutrients in any diet.
- o **Fatty Fish**
  - o **Nutritional Profile**: Salmon, mackerel, and sardines are sources of omega-3 fatty acids, protein, and vitamin D.
  - o **Health Benefits**: They help in the functioning of the brain, reduce inflammation in the body, as well as help the heart. Omega-3 fatty acids also play an important role in keeping cholesterol in check and may prevent chronic diseases.

Incorporating Nutrient-Dense Foods into Your Diet

- o **Smoothies**
  - o **Easy to Make**: Blend into a glass of smoothie some fresh spinach, blueberries, and almonds.
  - o **Variety**: It is recommended to try out different blends to ensure that you maintain your interest in consuming the smoothies. For a further boost of nutrients, one can add a scoop of protein powder or a spoonful of nut butter.
- o **Salads**
  - o **Versatile**: Prepare salads using fresh greens, nuts and seeds, and several different vegetables.
  - o **Protein Addition**: If you want your salad to be a full meal, then you can incorporate grilled chicken, tofu, or fatty fish. Try using homemade vinaigrette in dressing your salads, using healthy oils such as olive.
- o **Snacks**
  - o **Healthy Choices**: Instead of taking snacks from processed foods, take nuts, seeds, and berries.
  - o **Portion Control**: Ensure that you have smaller portions ready to prevent you from taking more than your required amount. It is recommended that you use

small containers or re-sealable bags to help you portion your foods and also make snacking easy.

- o **Main Meals**
  - o **Balanced Diet**: Ensure that the major meals are well balanced with nutrient-rich foods. Always make sure you are taking whole-grain foods with your vegetables and lean sources of protein for better nutrition.
  - o **Meal Prep**: Preparing meals in large quantities and then portioning them and freezing them can be very useful in that you will always have healthy meals available and save time.

Anti-inflammatory Diet

Inflammation is a process that is usually triggered by the immune system to counter any harm, although continuous inflammation can cause several diseases. This risk can be prevented by adopting an anti-inflammatory diet that is recommended for improved health. By choosing foods that fight inflammation, you can support your body's natural healing processes and improve your quality of life. This strategy not only relieves symptoms but also eliminates the sources of inflammation as well.

Inflammation

Inflammation is the body's defense mechanism against an injury or infection, although chronic inflammation can lead to arthritis, heart, and diabetes diseases.

- o **Causes**: Some of the causes of inflammation include the following: poor diet, stress, and lack of exercise. Other factors include environmental pollutants and certain behaviors such as smoking and alcoholism.
- o **Symptoms**: Some of the signs and manifestations are pain, swelling, and tiredness. It may also present itself in the form of gastrointestinal disorders, skin conditions, and recurrent infections.

Key Anti-inflammatory Foods

- • **Turmeric**
  - o **Active Ingredient**: Curcumin, the compound that is abundant in turmeric, is a potent anti-inflammatory agent.
  - o **Health Benefits**: Reduces joint pain, enhances brain function, and decreases the chances of getting a heart disease. It is possible to add turmeric to smoothies and teas or incorporate it as a spice to meals. Research also shows that when curcumin is taken together with black pepper, the absorption of curcumin is improved.
- • **Ginger**
  - o **Active Compounds**: Gingerol and shogaol have anti-inflammatory and antioxidant properties.

- **Health Benefits**: Aids in the management of pain, decreases stiffness in muscles, and enhances digestion. Ginger can be taken raw, in the form of tea, or included in some of the meals one takes.
- **Fatty Fish**
  - **Omega-3 Fatty Acids**: These are found in salmon, mackerel, and sardines and are good in reducing inflammation.
  - **Health Benefits**: Helps in the improvement of heart health, arthritis, and mental illnesses. It is recommended that you take fatty fish at least two times a week. Omega-3 supplements are also recommended for people who do not take fish products often.
- **Berries**
  - **Antioxidants**: Rich in anthocyanins, which have anti-inflammatory properties.
  - **Health Benefits**: Helps decrease the levels of LDL cholesterol, prevents the formation of blood clots, and increases the overall immune response. Berries can be added to smoothies and salads or can be eaten as raw food. Their natural sweetness can satisfy sugar cravings.
- **Leafy Greens**
  - **Nutrients**: Contain vitamins, minerals, and antioxidants that help in fighting inflammation.
  - **Health Benefits**: Boosts the immune system, enhances detoxification, and lowers the probability of developing chronic diseases. Add leafy greens to salads, juices, and other meals. Boiling and steaming of the vegetables should be done with a little bit of olive oil to help in the absorption of the nutrients.

Incorporating Anti-inflammatory Foods into Your Diet

- **Smoothies**
  - **Easy Addition**: Turmeric, ginger, and berries should be blended with the morning smoothie for a strong anti-inflammatory boost.
  - **Variety**: It is also recommended to add some variety to the ingredients of your smoothies and use different anti-inflammatory foods. One can up the nutritional value by adding some spinach or kale to the smoothie.
- **Salads**
  - **Versatile**: Make salads of green leaves, fatty fish, and a variety of colorful vegetables.
  - **Spices**: Add turmeric and ginger to your salad dressings because they are anti-inflammatory. Other greens, such as parsley and cilantro, are also good for use in salads, as they boost the flavor and the anti-inflammatory value.
- **Main Meals**
  - **Balanced Diet**: Ensure the main meals you take contain some of the A-list anti-inflammatory foods. Introduce whole grains with vegetables and lean proteins to have a balanced nutrition.
  - **Cooking Methods**: Use spices such as turmeric and ginger, which have anti-inflammatory properties, to make your dishes tastier and healthier. Choose

cooking methods that preserve nutrients to prepare your foods. For example, steam, grill, or bake.

- **Snacks**
  - **Healthy Choices**: Replace processed foods with foods that reduce inflammation, like berries, nuts, and seeds.
  - **Preparation**: Make ready portions of these snacks to make it easy to choose anti-inflammatory foods. Nut and seed-based snack bars that are prepared at home with the addition of dried fruits are a healthy snack choice.

Detoxification

Detoxification is a critical mechanism that enables the body to expel toxins and waste products and make you feel fresh and healthy. It is, therefore, possible to enhance your body's internal detoxification processes and a healthier life by observing proper nutrition. The consumption of detoxifying foods may assist in the elimination of wastes from your body, and increase energy as well as immunity.

Detoxification

Detoxification is the process by which the body rids itself of toxic substances and other waste products. This process involves the liver, kidneys, gastrointestinal tract, skin, and lungs.

- **Benefits**: Detoxification is said to improve digestion, increase energy levels, reduce weight, and improve one's skin.
- **Symptoms of Toxin Build-Up**: Fatigue, headache, indigestion, and skin rashes are some of the signs that you need to detox.

Key Detoxifying Foods

- **Leafy Greens**
  - **Nutritional Profile**: Spinach, kale, and arugula are packed with chlorophyll, vitamins, and minerals that help the liver to detoxify.
  - **Health Benefits**: These greens assist in removing heavy metals, pesticides, and other toxins from the body. They also help in digestion and proper bowel movement because of their high fiber content.
- **Cruciferous Vegetables**
  - **Nutritional Profile**: Some vegetables, such as broccoli, cauliflower, and Brussels sprouts, contain sulfur that facilitates the pathways of detoxification in the liver.
  - **Health Benefits**: These vegetables aid in the detoxification of the body since they can reduce the effects of toxins on the body. They also provide antioxidants that prevent the cells from getting damaged and reduce inflammation.
- **Citrus Fruits**
  - **Nutritional Profile**: Lemon, oranges, and grapefruits contain vitamin C and antioxidants that boost the immune system and detoxify the body.

- o **Health Benefits**: Citrus fruits activate the liver enzymes that aid in the metabolism of toxins into a form that can be expelled out of the body. They also assist in digestion and enhance the skin.
- **Berries**
  - o **Nutritional Profile**: Blueberries, strawberries, and raspberries contain antioxidants, vitamins, and fiber that can help in improving the diet.
  - o **Health Benefits**: Free radicals and inflammation are countered by the berries. They are rich in fiber, hence enhancing the proper digestion and expulsion of wastes from the body.
- **Garlic**
  - o **Nutritional Profile**: Garlic has sulfur compounds and selenium, which are effective in detoxifying the liver.
  - o **Health Benefits**: Garlic boosts the levels of the detoxification enzymes in the liver. It also has anti-microbial properties, which enable the expulsion of unhealthy bacteria and parasites from the gut.

Incorporating Detoxifying Foods into Your Diet

- **Smoothies**
  - o **Easy Addition**: Prepare a vitamin-packed green smoothie of spinach, strawberries, and oranges; great for detoxifying the body.
  - o **Variety**: Aim at varying the ingredients to make sure that the smoothies are not boring to you. One can also increase the detoxifying effects by placing a slice of ginger or one teaspoon of turmeric.
- **Salads**
  - o **Versatile**: Prepare salads consisting of a combination of green leafy vegetables, cruciferous vegetables, and colorful fruits.
  - o **Dressings**: To ensure that your salads are detox-friendly, use fresh lemon juice, olive oil, and herbs for your salad dressing. Sprinkle seeds or nuts into the batter to make it more nutritious and crunchy.
- **Main Meals**
  - o **Balanced Diet**: There should be incorporation of detoxifying foods in the main meals of the day. It is recommended that whole grain foods be taken together with vegetables and lean sources of protein for nutrition.
  - o **Cooking Methods**: To prepare your vegetables, steam, grill, or roast them as this will help in retaining the nutrients as well as the taste of the vegetables. Reduce the use of oils and processed seasonings.
- **Hydration**
  - o **Importance**: Water intake is very important in detoxifying as it aids in the elimination of toxins and other waste products.
  - o **Detox Water**: Infuse water with slices of lemon, cucumber, and mint for a refreshing and detoxifying beverage. Herbal teas such as dandelion and green tea may also help in detoxification.

Chapter 8

Kitchen Remedies

The main domestic sanctum, the kitchen, conceals the secrets that go beyond culinary delights. Within the pantry and spice rack are contained foods and seasonings that can bring about healing. Learning how to use your spices and condiments for healing can turn your regular tasks into healthy practices.

These natural remedies are quite effective in treating some of the minor illnesses that we encounter in our day-to-day lives, as well as boosting our immune system. It is time to unleash the curative qualities of things that you have at your disposal right now.

Common Kitchen Ingredients with Medicinal Properties

Most of the things we commonly add to our food to enhance the taste are more than just flavor enhancers. They are effective natural healers that have been in use right from ancient times, to cure different illnesses. Knowledge about the various beneficial effects of these ordinary ingredients will enable one to get the most out of them when it comes to nutrition and healing.

Garlic

- **Antibacterial and Antiviral Properties**: Garlic has a compound called allicin, which is known for overcoming various types of bacterial and viral infections.
  - o **Health Benefits**: It is possible to eat raw garlic to get rid of infections, reduce colds, and strengthen the immune system. It is a holistic approach to dealing with diseases without the use of synthetic antibiotics, which can have several side effects.
  - o **Usage**: Raw or lightly cooked garlic should be included in meals or taken in supplement form to get the full therapeutic potential of the herb.
- **Heart Health**: Galic also assists in lowering blood pressure and cholesterol levels and has beneficial effects on the heart.
  - o **Health Benefits**: Daily intake can reduce the chances of getting heart disease and improve the health of the heart.
  - o **Usage**: Add minced garlic in salads, soups, and sauces, or take garlic supplements to maintain heart health.

Turmeric: The Golden Spice

- **Anti-inflammatory Properties**: Turmeric has curcumin as its active anti-inflammatory agent.
    - o **Health Benefits**: Curcumin assists in the reduction of inflammation in the body, hence eradicating the symptoms of arthritis, digestive disorders, and other inflammatory diseases.
    - o **Usage**: Turmeric should be incorporated in cooking, blended into smoothies, or taken as golden milk to help reduce inflammation.
- **Antioxidant Effects**: Turmeric is endowed with antioxidant compounds that help shield the body from oxidative stress and free radicals.
    - o **Health Benefits**: They are important for general well-being and improve the efficiency of the body's immune system, as well as preventing various diseases.
    - o **Usage**: It is recommended that you add turmeric into your diet and make it a point to use it often for the protective benefits it has to offer.

Ginger

- **Digestive Health**: Ginger has a substance called gingerol, which helps in digestion and relieves gastrointestinal discomfort.
    - o **Health Benefits**: Ginger can reduce nausea, act as an antiemetic to an upset stomach, and promote digestion.
    - o **Usage**: For digestive ailments, it is recommended to consume ginger tea, include fresh ginger in your food, or chew sliced ginger.

- **Anti-inflammatory and Pain Relief**: It also has an anti-inflammatory effect which helps in alleviating muscle pain and soreness.
    - o **Health Benefits**: Regular consumption can be beneficial for people who suffer from chronic pain and improve recovery after physical exercise.
    - o **Usage**: It is recommended to use ginger in cooking, drink water with ginger in it, or take ginger supplements for pain relief.

Honey

- **Antibacterial and Wound Healing**: Honey has antimicrobial properties and can help in the healing of the wound.
    - o **Health Benefits**: Honey has antibacterial properties, and when applied to affected areas such as wounds and burns, it reduces the chances of infection and heals the area faster. Sore throat and cough can be eased by taking honey as it is also an expectorant.
    - o **Usage**: Apply raw honey topically for burns and other skin injuries, and take it internally in herbal teas to soothe sore throat.
- **Digestive Health**: Honey can enhance the digestive process effectively and is considered to be a prebiotic substance, supporting healthy gut bacteria.
    - o **Health Benefits**: Intake of honey can help in reducing the signs of digestive diseases, as well as enhance the composition of gut bacteria.

o **Usage**: Include honey in your diet by taking it as a natural sweetener in tea, smoothies, and other sweet dishes.

Lemon

- **Vitamin C and Antioxidants**: Lemons contain vitamin C and antioxidants that enhance the function of the immune system and the process of detoxification in the body.
    o **Health Benefits**: Some of the benefits include a boost in the immune system, better digestion, and better skin.
    o **Usage**: It is recommended that you start your day with a drink of warm water with a slice of lemon in it to help set your metabolism for the day and cleanse your body.
- **Alkalizing Effect**: Despite being acidic, lemons have a very strong alkaline-forming effect after digestion. Thus, they help the body regulate its pH.
    o **Health Benefits**: Keeping the body's PH levels in check is known to have positive effects on one's health and decrease the chances of developing diseases.
    o **Usage**: Lemon juice should be taken as a part of salads, drinks, and marinades to benefit from it.

Cinnamon

- **Blood Sugar Control**: Not only does cinnamon regulate the blood sugar level, but it also enhances insulin sensitivity.
    - o **Health Benefits**: Cinnamon can lower the chances of getting diabetes and manage blood sugar levels in diabetes patients.
    - o **Usage**: Add cinnamon to oats, yogurt, or coffee, or take it as a capsule to regulate diabetes.
- **Anti-inflammatory and Antioxidant Properties**: Cinnamon is another spice that has antioxidant properties and can help reduce inflammation.
    - o **Health Benefits**: These properties are useful in shielding the human body from oxidative stress as well as inflammation.
    - o **Usage**: Add cinnamon to your meals and recipes; incorporate it into your foods to increase the quality of your meals.

Apple Cider Vinegar

- **Digestive Health**: Apple cider vinegar (ACV) is good for digestion and helps in the right functioning of the stomach and other parts of the digestive system.
    - **Health Benefits**: ACV may help reduce the symptoms of indigestion, bloating, and acid reflux.
    - **Usage**: Take one tablespoon of ACV and mix it with water and then take it before meals, or add it to salads as a dressing.
- **Antimicrobial Properties**: ACV has inherent antimicrobial compounds that may help in preventing infections.
    - **Health Benefits**: The fact is that using ACV as a natural disinfectant can help avoid getting sick and enhance the condition of the skin.
    - **Usage**: It can be used as a facial toner or hair wash or taken internally to improve immune health.

DIY Health Elixirs and Tonics

Making your health tonics and elixirs at home is a rewarding way to enhance your wellness routine. These homemade remedies allow for a direct application of natural resources in treating ailments, depending on the individual's health state. From improving the immune system to improving digestion, home remedies and potions are a great way to look at improving one's health quickly and conveniently.

Ginger-Lemon Detox Tonic

- **Ingredients and Preparation**: Prepare a detoxifying tonic by combining fresh ginger, lemon juice, honey, and warm water.
  - **Recipe**: Ginger: peel and grate one small piece, lemon: one whole lemon juiced, honey: one teaspoon, warm water: one cup. It is best to allow it to steep for about five minutes before consumption.
  - **Benefits**: This tonic is very useful in cleansing the body, boosting the immune system, and aiding digestion. Ginger is beneficial to metabolism, while lemon possesses qualities that can detoxify the liver.
- **Usage**: This should be taken early in the morning to help jump-start the metabolism and detoxification process.
  - **Daily Routine**: Drinking this tonic daily will assist in keeping your digestive health in check and promote your overall health.

Turmeric-Golden Milk Elixir

- **Ingredients and Preparation**: Turmeric, ginger, cinnamon, black pepper, honey, and almond milk can be blended to make a warm drink with anti-inflammatory properties.
  - **Recipe**: One cup of almond milk should be warmed in a saucepan. Add to this a teaspoon of turmeric, a small piece of grated ginger, a pinch of cinnamon and black pepper, and honey. Mix it well and allow it to simmer for a few minutes.
  - **Benefits**: The benefits of this elixir include anti-inflammatory, immunomodulatory, and sedative properties. The combination of turmeric and black pepper promotes the absorption of curcumin, maximizing health benefits.
- **Usage**: This tonic should be consumed at night to help the body relax and have a good sleep.
  - **Evening Ritual**: Drinking this elixir every evening can be a good way to fight stress and sleep with better quality.

Apple Cider Vinegar Digestive Tonic

- **Ingredients and Preparation**: Mix apple cider vinegar with honey and warm water to make a good digestion remedy.
  - **Recipe**: Mix one tablespoon of apple cider vinegar with one teaspoon of honey and add it to one cup of warm water. Mix well until the honey has dissolved in the mixture.
  - **Benefits**: This tonic helps to digest food, regulate the acidity of the stomach, and promote healthy gut bacteria. Apple cider vinegar is also used to enhance digestion and reduce the level of bloating.
- **Usage**: Take this tonic before taking your meals to help in digestion and avoid cases of indigestion.
  - **Meal Preparation**: Incorporating this tonic into your pre-meal routine can help improve nutrient absorption and reduce digestive discomfort.

Cinnamon-Honey Immune Booster

- **Ingredients and Preparation**: Mix cinnamon with honey and warm water to get a natural remedy for boosting the immune system.
  - ○ **Recipe**: Put one teaspoon of cinnamon and one tablespoon of honey in a cup filled with warm water. Stir well until fully mixed.
  - ○ **Benefits**: This tonic increases the immunity of the body, decreases inflammation, and helps to fight against infections. Cinnamon and honey are potent antimicrobial and antioxidant agents when taken together.
- **Usage**: Take this tonic every day, but especially in the winter and when you are sick with a cold or the flu.
  - ○ **Seasonal Routine**: You can take this tonic every day in the winter and thus, avoid getting sick.

Beetroot-Lemon Liver Cleanse

- **Ingredients and Preparation**: Beetroot juice mixed with lemon juice and a pinch of salt can be taken as a liver detoxifying agent.
  - ○ **Recipe**: Squeeze one beetroot and blend with juice of one lemon, and a pinch of sea salt. Mix well and serve cold.
  - ○ **Benefits**: This tonic is used in the detoxification of the liver, increases energy levels, and promotes general well-being. Beetroot and lemon contain anti-oxidants that help detoxify the liver and also improve its functionality.
- **Usage**: This tonic should be taken once a week to maintain a healthy liver and detoxify the body.
  - ○ **Weekly Cleanse**: It is recommended to drink this tonic at least once a week to support the function of the liver and the body's detoxification mechanisms.

Nutritious Recipes for Wellness

1. Quinoa and Black Bean Salad

Preparation time: 10 minutes | **Cooking time:** 15 minutes | **Freezing time:** 0 minutes | **Total time:** 25 minutes | **Servings:** 4

Ingredients

- 2 tablespoons of olive oil
- Juice of 2 limes
- ¼ cup of chopped cilantro
- 1 diced avocado
- 1 cup of corn kernels
- 1 diced yellow bell pepper

- 1 diced red bell pepper

- 1 can of rinsed and drained black beans

- 1 cup of quinoa

- Pepper and salt

Cooking Instructions

1. Cook quinoa as per the instructions mentioned on the package and let it cool.
2. In a large bowl, mix the cooked quinoa, black beans, bell peppers, corn, avocado, and chopped cilantro.
3. In a small bowl, combine lime juice, olive oil, salt and pepper.
4. Put dressing over the salad and mix gently. Serve immediately or store in the refrigerator until ready to be consumed.

Nutritional information: Calories: 350 | **Protein:** 10g | **Carbohydrate:** 45g | **Fat:** 15g per serving

2. Avocado Toast with Poached Eggs

Preparation time: 10 minutes | **Cooking time**: 5 minutes | **Freezing time**: 0 minutes | **Total time**: 15 minutes | **Servings:** 2

Ingredients

- Red pepper flakes (this is optional)

- Pepper and salt

- 1 tablespoon of white vinegar

- 2 eggs

- 1 ripe avocado

- 2 slices whole grain bread

Cooking Instructions

1. Bake the bread slices to a golden-brown color.
2. Next, mash the avocado and spread it on the toast evenly.
3. Bring a pot of water to a simmer, then pour in white vinegar.
4. Beat each egg in a small bowl, and then slowly pour them into the simmering water. Poach for 3-4 minutes.
5. Remove eggs from the pan using a slotted spoon and place them on the avocado toast.
6. Sprinkle with salt, pepper, and red pepper flakes to taste, if desired.

Nutritional information: Calories: 300 | **Protein:** 12g | **Carbohydrate:** 30g | **Fat:** 15g per serving

3. Greek Yogurt and Berry Parfait

Preparation time: 5 minutes | **Cooking time**: 0 minutes | **Freezing time**: 0 minutes | **Total time**: 5 minutes | **Servings:** 2

Ingredients

- 2 tablespoons of honey
- ¼ cup of granola
- 1 cup of mixed berries (raspberries, strawberries, blueberries)
- 2 cups of Greek yogurt

Cooking Instructions

1. Take two serving glasses and garnish with a layer of Greek yogurt, mixed berries, then granola.
2. Pour honey on each of the parfait.
3. Serve immediately.

Nutritional information: Calories: 250 | **Protein:** 15g | **Carbohydrate:** 35g | **Fat:** 5g per serving

4. Spinach and Feta Stuffed Chicken Breast

Preparation time: 15 minutes | **Cooking time**: 30 minutes | **Freezing time**: 0 minutes | **Total time**: 45 minutes | **Servings:** 4

Ingredients

- 1 tablespoon of olive oil
- ¼ cup of chopped sun-dried tomatoes
- ½ cup of crumbled feta cheese
- 1 cup of chopped fresh spinach
- 4 skinless, boneless chicken breasts
- Pepper and salt

Cooking Instructions

1. Heat the oven to 375 degrees Fahrenheit or 190 degrees Celsius.
2. Make an incision through the thickness of the meat to form a pocket.
3. To make the filling, mix the spinach, crumbled feta cheese, and sun-dried tomatoes in a bowl.
4. Place the spinach filling in the center of each chicken breast and then fix it with toothpicks.
5. In a skillet, heat the olive oil with the heat on medium-high. Pan-fry the chicken breasts for 2-3 minutes on each side.

6. Remove chicken and transfer to a baking dish. Bake for another 20-25 minutes or until it is cooked through.
7. Remove toothpicks before serving.

Nutritional information: Calories: 350 | **Protein:** 30g | **Carbohydrate:** 5g | **Fat:** 20g per serving

5. Sweet Potato and Black Bean Chili

Preparation time: 10 minutes | **Cooking time:** 30 minutes | **Freezing time:** 0 minutes | **Total time:** 40 minutes | **Servings:** 6

Ingredients

- 1 teaspoon of cumin
- 1 tablespoon of chili powder
- 2 cups of vegetable broth
- 3 minced cloves of garlic
- 1 diced onion
- 1 diced bell pepper
- 1 can of diced tomatoes
- 2 large sweet potatoes, diced and peeled
- 1 can of black beans, rinsed and drained
- Pepper and salt
- 1 tablespoon of olive oil

Cooking Instructions

1. In a large pot, sauté olive oil under medium heat. Put onion and garlic and fry until they are browned.
2. Add sweet potatoes, bell pepper, and spices. Cook for 5 minutes.
3. Add the black beans, diced tomatoes, and vegetable broth to the mixture. Bring to a boil and then decrease heat, then simmer for 20-25 minutes until sweet potatoes are soft.
4. Season with salt and pepper to your desire. Serve hot.

Nutritional information: Calories: 280 | **Protein:** 10g | **Carbohydrate:** 45g | **Fat:** 5g per serving

6. Baked Salmon with Lemon and Dill

Preparation time: 5 minutes | **Cooking time:** 20 minutes | **Freezing time:** 0 minutes | **Total time:** 25 minutes | **Servings:** 4

Ingredients

- 1 tablespoon of olive oil

- 2 tablespoons of chopped fresh dill

- 2 thinly sliced lemons

- 4 salmon fillets

- Pepper and salt

Cooking Instructions

1. Preheat the oven to 375°F (190°C).
2. Put the salmon fillets on a baking sheet lined with parchment paper.
3. Pour olive oil over the fillets and then sprinkle it with salt and black pepper.
4. Place lemon slices and dill on top of the salmon.
5. Bake for 20 minutes or until the salmon is cooked through to the center.

Nutritional information: Calories: 350 | **Protein:** 30g | **Carbohydrate:** 2g | **Fat:** 25g per serving

7. Chickpea and Avocado Salad

Preparation time: 10 minutes | **Cooking time**: 0 minutes | **Freezing time**: 0 minutes | **Total time**: 10 minutes | **Servings:** 4

Ingredients

- 2 tablespoons of olive oil

- Juice of 1 lemon

- ¼ cup of chopped fresh parsley

- 1 finely chopped red onion

- 1 diced cucumber

- 1 diced avocado

- 1 can of chickpeas, rinsed and drained

- Pepper and salt

Cooking Instructions

1. Chickpeas, avocado, cucumber, red onion, and parsley should be added to a large bowl.
2. In a small bowl, combine the lemon juice, olive oil, salt and pepper.
3. Pour dressing over salad and mix gently. Serve immediately.

Nutritional information: Calories: 250 | **Protein:** 7g | **Carbohydrate:** 25g | **Fat:** 15g per serving

8. Greek Yogurt Chicken Salad

Preparation time: 15 minutes | **Cooking time**: 0 minutes | **Freezing time**: 0 minutes | **Total time**: 15 minutes | **Servings**: 4

Ingredients

- 1 tablespoon of Dijon mustard
- ¼ cup of chopped walnuts
- ½ cup of halved red grapes
- ½ cup of chopped celery
- 1 cup of Greek yogurt
- 2 cups of cooked and shredded chicken breast
- Pepper and salt

Cooking Instructions

1. Mix the chicken, Greek yogurt, celery, grapes, walnuts, and Dijon mustard in a large bowl.

2. Stir and season with salt and pepper to taste.

3. Enjoy hot or store in the refrigerator until you are ready to eat it.

Nutritional information: Calories: 200 | **Protein:** 25g | **Carbohydrate:** 10g | **Fat:** 8g per serving

9. Lentil and Vegetable Soup

Preparation time: 10 minutes | **Cooking time**: 40 minutes | **Freezing time**: 0 minutes | **Total time**: 50 minutes | **Servings**: 6

Ingredients

- 1 teaspoon of cumin
- 1 teaspoon of thyme
- 6 cups of vegetable broth
- 1 can of diced tomatoes
- 3 cloves of minced garlic
- 1 diced onion
- 2 diced celery stalks
- 2 diced carrots
- 1 cup of rinsed lentils
- Pepper and salt

- 1 tablespoon of olive oil

Cooking Instructions

1. In a large pot, heat olive oil until it simmers on the stove at medium heat. Put onion and garlic and stir fry until aromatic.
2. Put the carrots, celery, and spices in. Cook for 5 minutes.
3. Add lentils, tomatoes, and vegetable stock to the pot. Stir well and let it boil, then reduce the heat and let it simmer for 30-35 minutes until the lentils are soft.
4. Add salt and pepper to your desired preference. Serve hot.

Nutritional information: Calories: 200 | **Protein:** 12g | **Carbohydrate:** 30g | **Fat:** 4g per serving

10. Quinoa and Veggie Stir-Fry

Preparation time: 10 minutes | **Cooking time**: 15 minutes | **Freezing time**: 0 minutes | **Total time**: 25 minutes | **Servings:** 4

Ingredients

- ¼ cup of chopped green onions

- 1 tablespoon of olive oil

- 2 tablespoons of soy sauce

- 2 cloves of minced garlic

- 1 cup of broccoli florets

- 1 sliced zucchini

- 1 sliced yellow bell pepper

- 1 sliced red bell pepper

- 1 cup of quinoa

Cooking Instructions

1. Follow the package instructions on how to prepare quinoa and cook it. Let cool.
2. Turn the heat to medium-high and heat olive oil in a large skillet. Put garlic in and stir fry until the garlic is brown.
3. As for the vegetables, add the bell peppers, the zucchini, and the broccoli. Stir for 5-7 minutes until vegetables are cooked.
4. Add in cooked quinoa and soy sauce. Cook for 2-3 minutes more.
5. For garnishing, sprinkle some chopped green onions on it and serve hot.

Nutritional information: Calories: 300 | **Protein:** 10g | **Carbohydrate:** 45g | **Fat:** 10g per serving

11. Berry and Spinach Smoothie

Preparation time: 5 minutes | **Cooking time**: 0 minutes | **Freezing time**: 0 minutes | **Total time**: 5 minutes | **Servings:** 2

Ingredients

- 1 tablespoon of chia seeds
- 1 cup of almond milk
- 1 banana
- 1 cup of mixed berries (raspberries, blueberries, strawberries)
- 1 cup of spinach leaves

Cooking Instructions

1. Put all the ingredients in a blender.
2. Blend until it is smooth and creamy.
3. Serve immediately.

Nutritional information: Calories: 180 | **Protein:** 5g | **Carbohydrate:** 35g | **Fat:** 3g per serving

12. Cauliflower Rice Bowl

Preparation time: 10 minutes | **Cooking time**: 10 minutes | **Freezing time**: 0 minutes | **Total time**: 20 minutes | **Servings:** 4

Ingredients

- ¼ cup of chopped cilantro
- 1 avocado, sliced
- 1 cup of halved cherry tomatoes
- 1 cup of cooked chickpeas
- 1 head of rice-sized grated cauliflower pieces
- Juice of 1 lime
- Pepper and salt
- 1 tablespoon of olive oil

Cooking Instructions

1. In a large skillet, heat olive oil over medium heat. Stir in cauliflower rice and cook for 5-7 minutes until softened.
2. Mix cooked cauliflower rice, chickpeas, cherry tomatoes, avocado, and cilantro in a bowl.
3. Sprinkle salt and pepper drizzle with lime juice. Toss to combine and serve at once.

Nutritional information: Calories: 220 | **Protein:** 6g | **Carbohydrate:** 25g | **Fat:** 12g per serving

13. Spaghetti Squash with Marinara Sauce

Preparation time: 10 minutes | **Cooking time**: 40 minutes | **Freezing time**: 0 minutes | **Total time**: 50 minutes | **Servings:** 4

Ingredients

- ¼ cup of grated Parmesan cheese
- 2 cups of marinara sauce
- 1 spaghetti squash
- Pepper and salt
- Fresh basil for garnish
- 1 tablespoon of olive oil

Cooking Instructions

1. Preheat oven to 375°F (190°C). Cut Spaghetti Squash and scoop out the seed!
2. Rub the cut part with olive oil, salt, and pepper, then lay it on a baking sheet.
3. Bake for 35-40 minutes or until soft.
4. Scrape the flesh with a fork to make spaghetti strands.
5. Heat the marinara in a small pot over medium heat. Serve over spaghetti squash and top with Parmesan cheese and fresh basil.

Nutritional information: Calories: 200 | **Protein:** 6g | **Carbohydrate:** 35g | **Fat:** 6g per serving

14. Avocado and Chickpea Sandwich

Preparation time: 10 minutes | **Cooking time**: 0 minutes | **Freezing time**: 0 minutes | **Total time**: 10 minutes | **Servings:** 2

Ingredients

- 1 cup of mixed greens
- 4 slices of whole-grain bread
- Pepper and salt
- 1 teaspoon of garlic powder
- 1 tablespoon of lemon juice
- 1 mashed avocado
- 1 can of rinsed and drained chickpeas

Cooking Instructions

1. Mash chickpeas and avocado together in a bowl.
2. Mix well with lemon juice, garlic powder, salt and pepper.
3. Spread some mixture onto two pieces of bread. After adding the mixed greens, top with the remaining bread slices.
4. Serve immediately.

Nutritional information: Calories: 300 | **Protein:** 10g | **Carbohydrate:** 45g | **Fat:** 12g per serving

15. Zucchini Noodles with Pesto

Preparation time: 10 minutes | **Cooking time**: 5 minutes | **Freezing time**: 0 minutes | **Total time**: 15 minutes | **Servings:** 4

Ingredients

- 2 cloves of garlic
- ¼ cup of olive oil
- ¼ cup of grated Parmesan cheese
- ¼ cup of pine nuts
- 1 cup of fresh basil leaves
- 4 zucchinis, spiralized into noodles
- Pepper and salt

Cooking Instructions

1. Combine the basil, pine nuts, Parmesan cheese, and garlic with a pinch of salt and pepper in a food processor. Pulse until finely chopped.
2. Process, slowly adding olive oil in a thin stream as you go until the mixture is smooth and creamy.
3. Place a large skillet over medium heat. Add zucchini noodles and cook for 2-3 minutes until slightly tender.
4. Toss the zucchini noodles with pesto and serve immediately

Nutritional information: Calories: 250 | **Protein:** 8g | **Carbohydrate:** 10g | **Fat:** 20g per serving

Part IV

Complementary Therapies

Chapter 9

Mind-Body Connection

Your mind and body share a dynamic relationship that shapes our overall health. When one suffers, the other often follows, creating a ripple effect that can impact every facet of your life. The connection between thoughts, emotions, and physical well-being is profound, often dictating how you navigate daily challenges. Embracing this interdependence can unlock new pathways to healing and balance.

Importance of Stress Management

Stress is an inevitable part of life, but how you manage it can make all the difference to your health. By addressing stress effectively, you create a buffer against its harmful effects, fostering resilience and well-being. Let's explore practical strategies to manage stress, bringing harmony to your mind and body.

Stress is the body's reaction to any change that requires an adjustment or response. It can be physical, emotional, or mental. Understanding what triggers your stress is the first step toward managing it. There are two main types of stress: acute and chronic. Acute stress is short-term and often related to immediate threats or pressures. Chronic stress is long-term and can have more serious health implications if not addressed.

Stress Symptoms

- **Physical Symptoms**: Stress often manifests physically. You might experience headaches, muscle tension, fatigue, or digestive issues. Recognizing these signs early can help you take action before stress takes a heavier toll.

- **Emotional Symptoms**: Emotionally, stress can lead to feelings of anxiety, depression, irritability, or feeling overwhelmed. Being aware of these emotional signals is crucial for managing your mental health effectively.

Techniques for Managing Stress

- **Mindfulness Practices**: Mindfulness involves being present in the moment without judgment. It helps reduce stress by allowing you to focus on the here and now rather than worrying about the past or future.

- **Meditation Benefits**: Regular meditation can significantly reduce stress levels. It promotes relaxation, increases self-awareness, and can lead to a more positive outlook on life.

- **Exercise as a Stress Reliever**: Physical activity is a powerful stress reliever. It boosts the production of endorphins, the body's natural mood lifters. Even a short walk can make a big difference.

- **Yoga and Tai Chi**: These practices combine physical movement with deep breathing and mindfulness, making them effective for reducing stress and improving overall health.

- **Deep Breathing**: Deep breathing exercises can help calm your mind and body. Techniques like diaphragmatic breathing or the 4-7-8 method can quickly reduce stress levels.

- **Progressive Muscle Relaxation**: This technique involves tensing and then slowly relaxing each muscle group in your body. It helps release physical tension and promotes a sense of relaxation.

- **Nutrition and Hydration**: Eating a balanced diet and staying hydrated can impact your stress levels. Nutrient-rich foods support brain function and energy levels, making you more resilient to stress.

- **Adequate Sleep**: Quality sleep is essential for stress management. Establishing a regular sleep routine and creating a restful environment can improve sleep quality and reduce stress.

- **Social Connections**: Strong social connections can act as a buffer against stress. Spending time with friends and family provides emotional support and helps you feel less isolated.

- **Professional Help**: Sometimes, professional help is necessary. Therapists and counselors can provide strategies and support for managing stress and its effects.

Relaxation Techniques

Engaging in hobbies and activities you enjoy can provide a much-needed distraction from stress. Creative activities, in particular, can be very therapeutic. Spending time in nature has been shown to reduce stress. Whether it's a walk in the park or a weekend camping trip, nature can provide a calming escape from daily pressures.

Effective time management can reduce stress by helping you feel more in control. Prioritize tasks and break them down into manageable steps to avoid feeling overwhelmed. Learn to say no when necessary. Setting boundaries can prevent burnout and help maintain a healthy work-life balance.

Keeping a gratitude journal can shift your focus from what's stressing you to what you're thankful for. This simple practice can improve your mood and reduce stress. Positive affirmations can boost your confidence and help you approach stressful situations with a more positive mindset.

Meditation and Mindfulness Techniques

Meditation and mindfulness are powerful tools that bring a sense of calm and clarity to the chaos of modern life. By training your mind to focus and be present, you can significantly reduce stress and improve your overall well-being. Let's explore various techniques that can help you cultivate a mindful, meditative practice.

Mindfulness is the practice of paying attention to the present moment without judgment. It's about observing your thoughts, feelings, and sensations as they are without trying to change or suppress them. Regular mindfulness practice can reduce stress, enhance emotional regulation, and improve focus. It encourages a balanced perspective and a deeper connection with yourself and your surroundings.

Basic Meditation Techniques

Focused Attention Meditation

- **Breath Awareness**: This technique involves focusing on your breath. Pay attention to the sensation of air entering and leaving your nostrils or the rise and fall of your chest. When your mind wanders, gently bring it back to your breath.

- **Counting Breaths**: Count each breath cycle to maintain focus. Start with a count of four and gradually increase. This helps anchor your attention and quiet the mind.

Body Scan Meditation

- **Full Body Scan**: Lie down or sit comfortably. Slowly bring your attention to different parts of your body, starting from your toes and moving up to your head. Notice any sensations, tension, or relaxation.

- **Tension Release**: As you scan each body part, consciously release any tension you find. This promotes relaxation and helps you become more aware of physical stress.

Guided Visualization

- **Imagery**: Guided visualization involves imagining a peaceful scene or situation. This could be a serene beach, a quiet forest, or any place that brings you a sense of calm.

- **Sensory Engagement**: Engage all your senses in the visualization. Feel the warmth of the sun, hear the sound of waves, and smell the fresh air. This immersive experience can deeply relax and refresh your mind.

Advanced Mindfulness Practices

Loving-Kindness Meditation (Metta)

- **Generating Kindness**: Start by focusing on yourself, silently repeating phrases like "May I be happy, may I be healthy." Gradually extend these wishes to others, including loved ones, acquaintances, and even those with whom you have conflicts.

- **Expanding Compassion**: This practice enhances empathy and compassion, fostering positive emotions and reducing stress and resentment.

Mindful Walking

- **Awareness in Movement**: Practice mindfulness while walking by paying attention to the sensation of your feet touching the ground, the movement of your body, and your surroundings.

- **Rhythm and Breath**: Coordinate your breath with your steps. This synchrony can create a meditative rhythm that calms your mind and grounds you in the present moment.

Integrating Mindfulness into Daily Life

Mindful Eating

- **Savoring Each Bite**: Eat slowly and mindfully, paying attention to the taste, texture, and aroma of your food. This practice can enhance your enjoyment of meals and improve digestion.

- **Gratitude for Food**: Reflect on the journey of your food from farm to table. This awareness can deepen your appreciation and mindfulness during meals.

Mindful Listening

- **Active Listening**: When engaging in conversations, focus fully on the speaker without planning your response. Notice their words, tone, and body language.

- **Empathetic Engagement**: This practice can improve your relationships by fostering deeper connections and understanding.

Overcoming Challenges in Meditation

Dealing with Distractions

- **Acceptance of Thoughts**: Instead of fighting distractions, acknowledge them and gently bring your focus back to your meditation. Remember, it's normal for the mind to wander.

- **Creating a Routine**: Establish a regular meditation practice. Consistency can help train your mind and make meditation more natural and effective.

Managing Time

- **Short Sessions**: Start with short meditation sessions, even just five minutes a day. Gradually increase the duration as you become more comfortable.

- **Incorporating Mindfulness**: Integrate mindfulness into daily activities, like brushing your teeth or washing dishes. This approach can make it easier to maintain a consistent practice.

Yoga and Tai Chi for Overall Well-being

Yoga and Tai Chi are ancient practices that have stood the test of time for a reason. They offer profound benefits for both mind and body, making them powerful tools for achieving overall well-being. By integrating these practices into your routine, you can enhance your physical health, mental clarity, and emotional balance.

Benefits of Yoga

- **Flexibility and Strength**: Yoga poses, or asanas, stretch and strengthen various muscle groups. This not only increases flexibility but also builds muscle strength, supporting overall physical health.

- **Stress Reduction**: Yoga incorporates deep breathing and meditation, which can significantly reduce stress levels. Practicing yoga regularly can help calm the mind and reduce the physical effects of stress on the body.

Types of Yoga

- **Hatha Yoga**: This is a gentle introduction to the basic yoga postures. Hatha yoga is great for beginners and focuses on slow, gentle movements and breathing.

- **Vinyasa Yoga**: This style involves a sequence of poses that flow smoothly into one another. It's more dynamic and can provide a good cardiovascular workout in addition to its mental and physical benefits.

Benefits of Tai Chi

- **Balance and Coordination**: Tai Chi involves slow, deliberate movements that improve balance and coordination. This can be especially beneficial for older adults or those recovering from injuries.

- **Mental Focus**: The slow, focused movements of Tai Chi require concentration and mindfulness. This practice can help improve mental clarity and focus, reducing anxiety and promoting a sense of calm.

Types of Tai Chi

- **Yang Style**: The most popular form, Yang style, is characterized by slow, graceful movements. It's ideal for beginners and provides a full-body workout that's gentle yet effective.

- **Chen Style**: This is a more vigorous form of Tai Chi that includes faster movements and jumps. It's suited for those looking for a more challenging workout that still incorporates the principles of Tai Chi.

Integrating Yoga and Tai Chi into Daily Life

Starting your day with a yoga or Tai Chi session can set a positive tone for the day. It energizes the body and calms the mind, preparing you to face daily challenges with grace and ease. Practicing yoga or Tai Chi in the evening can help you unwind from the stresses of the day. It promotes relaxation and improves sleep quality, making it easier to get a restful night's sleep.

Yoga and Tai Chi complement each other well. While yoga focuses more on stretching and flexibility, Tai Chi emphasizes balance and fluid movement. Practicing both can provide a well-rounded approach to physical and mental well-being. Both practices enhance the mind-body connection, making you more aware of your physical and mental state. This awareness can help you better manage stress and improve your overall health.

To reap the full benefits of yoga and Tai Chi, consistency is crucial. Even short daily sessions can make a significant difference in your overall well-being. Joining a yoga or Tai Chi class can provide support and motivation. It's also a great way to meet like-minded individuals who are on a similar wellness journey.

Chapter 10

Homeopathy and Beyond

The desire to use natural therapies has always been inspiring for humanity for many centuries. Studying such practices helps to discover the valuable experience of ancestors in the field of health and healing. It is for this reason that many have embraced practices that include holistic and person-centered care. As we explore these methods, we find not only a cure but a way of life that is in tune with our primal instincts of harmony. This chapter will, therefore, seek to bring light to these practices, give a modern spin to ageless proverbs, and make sense of why they are still relevant today.

Homeopathic Principles

The Principle of Similars

You and I have an inborn ability to recover and grow, an aspect that the principle of similars makes us realize. This principle of homeopathy, also known as the principle of similia, or "let likes treat likes," means that the remedy capable of producing symptoms in healthy individuals can cure symptoms in sick individuals. Consider the example of a red onion: It is something that can make your eyes water and your nose run.

Also, based on the principle of similars, a homeopathic remedy derived from red onion known as Allium cepa may be used to cure a cold or an allergy with similar symptoms. This idea, which might sound counterintuitive, has its origin in the Hippocratic school of medicine in ancient Greece which stated diseases could be treated by substances that caused similar changes in the body.

- **Historical Roots**: The idea of "similia similibus curentur" is not new. The famous ancient Greek physician Hippocrates, known as the father of medicine, stated that some diseases can be cured with substances that cause the same symptoms. This principle was later on developed and expanded by Samuel Hahnemann, who founded homeopathy. In the 1790s, Hahnemann's experiments allowed him to determine that shaking and diluting substances could increase the therapeutic effects of substances but reduce their side effects, which created homeopathy.

- **Practical Applications**: The current homeopaths dedicate a lot of time to determining the peculiarities of each patient's complaint to prescribe them the correct remedy. This approach to treatment makes it possible for even two people who are suffering from similar diseases to be treated differently. For example, a patient with insomnia will use Coffea cruda, while another patient with the same condition will use Nux vomica, depending on the patient's general health status. This course of treatment is prescribed for each patient to stimulate the body's self-healing processes.

Dilution and Potentization

Potentization is a central process in homeopathy, which is based on the process of serial dilution and succussion, which is vigorous shaking. It is said that this technique enhances the curative properties of the base material while reducing or eradicating the poisonous quality. Opponents claim that dilutions of this nature reduce the remedies to placebo since no particles of the original substance are present. Nonetheless, according to homeopaths, it is the energy of the substance that is left on the sucrose tablet that is responsible for the curative effects.

- **Process of Potentization**: Potentization means dilution of a substance followed by succussion and this can be done many times. For instance, a remedy that has the label 30C has been diluted 1 part in 100, thirty consecutive times. This process is considered to increase the therapeutic effect of the remedy since it charges the solution. It was a major discovery made by Samuel Hahnemann that indicated that it was possible to minimize the side effects of substances while increasing their curative abilities, a discovery that has since come to define homeopathy.

- **Energetic Imprint Theory**: The discussion of potentization is mainly related to the idea of an energetic imprint. According to homeopaths, even if the substance is diluted to the extent where no molecules of the substance can be detected, it influences the body's vital force due to its 'memory.' This claim has been supplemented by such testimonies and accounts from patients, which often show how highly diluted remedies have provided positive health outcomes. For instance, a person with chronic migraines will be able to use a remedy diluted to 200C and eventually get fewer headaches and become better.

The Holistic Approach

Homeopathy stands out due to the approach that this type of medicine considers the individual as a whole, not focusing on specific symptoms. This philosophy accords with the principles of holism that assert that the physical, the emotional, and the mental need to be treated as a single entity to be cured. According to lifestyle, emotional state, and physical condition, homeopaths can attempt to bring the body back into harmony and activate the healing abilities of the organism.

- **Whole-Person Care**: During the conversation, a homeopath tries to obtain as many details as possible about a person's life, including diet, stress, emotions, and health history. This holistic strategy proves useful in choosing the right intervention that fits the patient's symptom presentation. For instance, a person with anxiety and stomach problems will be given a remedy such as Argentum nitricum depending on the manifestation of symptoms and general state of health.

- **Individualized Remedies**: In this respect, homeopathy is different from conventional medicine, where the patient gets a specific disease that is treated with a specific medicine. This is a form of care that recognizes that people get ill in different ways. Two people with eczema might receive different treatments: one may need Graphite if the skin is tough and secreting a thick, slimy coating, while the other may require Sulphur as heat aggravates the condition. This approach is expected to focus on the actual problem that is causing the ailment as opposed to just solving the symptoms.

s

Common Homeopathic Remedies

Homeopathic remedies are made of natural substances, and that is why they can work gently on an individual's body. These remedies are for most of the diseases that people experience in their day-to-day lives, whether they are acute or chronic. To give a brief idea about this kind of practice, it is essential to look at some of the widely used homeopathic remedies and their applications.

Arnica Montana

- **Uses and Benefits**: Arnica Montana, also referred to as Arnica, is among the most popular homeopathic remedies across the globe. It is extracted from the Arnica plant, which is a yellow mountain flower. Arnica is mainly used to address physical injury and inflammation, including bruises, sprains, and muscle pain. It is also useful for decreasing inflammation and decrease pain following operations or dental work. Athletes and other physically active people always have Arnica handy to help them with the healing process of their injuries.

- **Personal Experiences**: Imagine that after climbing a mountain, your muscles are sore, and you have a bruise on your knee from a recent fall. When you apply Arnica, it will help lessen the pain and the intensity of the bruise so that you can begin moving again. Some have described how Arnica has aided them in their fast healing from falls and knocks, and they always ensure they have this remedy with them as a first aid remedy.

Nux Vomica

- **Uses and Benefits**: Nux Vomica is obtained from seeds of Strychnos nux-vomica tree. This remedy is commonly employed for gastrointestinal problems that are usually associated with eating, drinking alcohol, or consumption of stimulating beverages such as coffee. Nux Vomica is seen to be effective in cases of symptoms like heartburn, nausea, and bloating. It is also useful for those who have stress-related intestinal colic and headaches.

- **Personal Experiences**: Suppose you have overindulged in some food and are now struggling with indigestion and a severe headache. You can try taking Nux Vomica. It will surely make you feel better by calming your stomach. This remedy is useful during the holiday season or after nights of overindulgence because the body can easily regain its balance.

Ignatia Amara

- **Uses and Benefits**: Ignatia Amara, which is obtained from the seeds of the St. Ignatius bean, is commonly used in cases of mental issues. In this way, it is especially useful in cases of grief, anxiety, and when someone is in a state of emotional shock. For patients who have complaints such as a lump in the throat, sighing, or mood changes, Ignatia might help. It is also helpful to take this remedy if one struggles with disappointment or loss.

- **Personal Experiences**: Imagine this: You are sitting in your class after a breakup or after the loss of a loved one. You are sad and cannot concentrate. Ignatia can also alleviate suffering and give you a sense of peace so that you can sort out your feelings in a healthier manner. Some people have described how Ignatia led them through a time of great emotional suffering and provided comfort when nobody else did.

Belladonna

- **Uses and Benefits**: Belladonna is derived from the plant called deadly nightshade. However, when homeopathically prepared, Belladonna is not poisonous and is very useful in the management of acute conditions that are rapidly developing and marked by intense symptoms. It is often used in the treatment of high fever, pulsating headache, and conditions that cause inflammation. Complaints that are acute and characterized by redness, heat, and throbbing are treated with Belladonna.

- **Personal Experiences**: Suppose you wake up at night feeling sick with a very high temperature and a very bad headache. Belladonna can give swift relief and may rapidly bring the fever down and ease the headache so that you can sleep and recuperate. Parents even today have Belladonna in their homes because it is a ready remedy for those unexpected illnesses that children are prone to at night.

Rhus Toxicodendron

- Uses and Benefits: Rhus Toxicodendron or Rhus Tox is made from the poison ivy plant, which is well known. This is used as first-line treatment in conditions that have stiffness and where movement relieves the pain. This homeopathic remedy is prescribed for arthritis, back pain, skin rash, and itching that becomes worse when the patient is immobile and relieved by activity.

- **Personal Experiences**: Think about getting out of bed one morning and finding your fingers and toes clicking like a rusty gate but loosening up as you begin to walk around. Rhus Tox can be used to alleviate the stiffness and pain thereby enabling one to go on with your activities. Rhus Tox is a savior for many people with chronic joint problems or those who may have overdone it and need relief to carry on with their daily activities.

Acupuncture and Acupressure: Balancing Energy

Acupuncture and acupressure, which are from Traditional Chinese Medicine (TCM), have a strong belief in the flow of energy called Qi in the human body. It circulates in channels known as meridians and regulating this is the primary approach to health. These practices involve the application of pressure on specific areas of the body to bring about balance hence treating various diseases and disorders.

Qi and Meridians

In TCM, Qi is the energy that is said to permeate every living thing and is vital for the body to function properly. It is thought to control physical, emotive, cognitive, and spiritual health. The body operates optimally if Qi circulates well in the body, and this is the reason why the Chinese believe that Qi is the key to health. However, when there is an obstruction, or the flow is not normal, there is disease and pain. Acupuncture and acupressure are effective in that they seek to unblock the pathways and reroute the flow of Qi to bring the body back into balance and, thus, health.

The body is divided into zones that are called meridians, which are channels that Qi circulates through. They are twelve in number and are associated with the organs and functions of the body. Through the stimulation of specific points along these lines, the practitioner is thus able to help harmonize energy and treat numerous ailments. For instance, when the Lung meridian is being massaged, certain points might be used to treat respiratory problems.

Acupuncture Techniques

- **Insertion of Needles**: Acupuncture is a form of therapy that entails the use of thin needles on the skin at particular points on the body. These needles are generally retained in the body for about fifteen to thirty minutes. The feeling can range from a tickle to numbness or a feeling of being weighted down at the targeted acupuncture points. The objective of this is to increase the circulation of Qi and thus restore growth and health to the body.

- **Benefits of Acupuncture**: This technique has been used to treat and control pain and stress and even enhance general well-being. Some studies show that acupuncture is effective for chronic pain, migraines, anxiety, and insomnia. For instance, a study on chronic lower back pain showed that participants who underwent acupuncture had considerably less pain than those who received conventional treatments.

- **Electroacupuncture**: A further development of acupuncture, electroacupuncture entails the use of electric current to the inserted needles. This technique can complement normal acupuncture in improving the health condition of patients, especially in cases of pain and muscular injury. The patients using this method complain of a much stronger feeling and deeper outcomes.

Acupressure Techniques

- **Pressure Application**: Acupressure applies finger pressure on the body instead of needles as a means of applying pressure on specific points. This technique is relatively easier for those who might have some anxiety towards needles. In this process, the practitioners use their fingers, palms, elbows, or some other instrument on the patient's body and apply pressure to regulate the Qi and release tension.

- **Self-Care with Acupressure**: A major benefit of acupressure is that it can be done without the assistance of a professional. It is important to note that acquiring a few fundamental points makes it possible for any person to address stress levels, minimize pain, and improve well-being without the help of a specialist. For instance, the LI4 point on the hand can be pressed to cure headaches and relieve stress.

- **Benefits of Acupressure**: Like in the case of acupuncture, acupressure is effective in treating several ailments such as nausea, fatigue, and chronic pain. The most common benefits include relief from tension headaches and muscle rigidity. Research indicates that acupressure can help in the decrease of the intensity and the frequency of migraines thus offering an alternative to medicine.

Combining Acupuncture and Acupressure

- **Synergistic Effects**: Synergistically, acupuncture, and acupressure can work to make the two treatments more effective. For instance, getting acupuncture for chronic pain while doing acupressure on your own would result in better and lasting relief. This combined approach also can be modified to the specific client's needs, thereby enhancing the effectiveness of each modality.

- **Holistic Health Benefits**: Both techniques aim at the regulation of Qi and the health of the body and are based on the same principles. When combined, they can deal with more problems in a better way than when each of them is used alone. For example, if a person is experiencing chronic pain, acupuncture might target that problem, while acupressure can be used regularly.

Emotional and Mental Health Benefits

- **Stress Reduction**: Acupuncture as well as acupressure, was found to have a positive effect on stress and anxiety levels. Many of these techniques help to reduce tension and achieve a state of harmony, which can have beneficial effects on the emotional state of the individual. Some patients have complained of increased feeling of balance and less clutter after the treatments.

- **Mood Regulation**: Stimulating certain areas can also be used to change the mood and overall mental state of a person. For instance, there are acupuncture points such as Yintang that are situated between the eyebrows and are commonly used to reduce anxiety and enhance sleep. This, in turn, can help in achieving better moods and an enhanced perspective of life.

Chapter 11

Balancing Your Life

Life is a balancing act and, in many instances, it is hard to achieve balance, but without it, things are out of order. Every day is a new day with different difficulties and possibilities. It is like trying to maintain a balance that sometimes seems impossible. Achieving this balance is not just about time management; it is about caring for each aspect of you. Think of a life that is more focused on the physical, mental, and emotional well-being of an individual, and all these aspects complement each other. What is more, this harmony is not only possible but also achievable in your case. Now, let's discuss the elements that may lead to having a balanced and satisfying life with the help of herbal remedies.

The Pillars of Wellness: Physical, Mental, and Emotional Health

Physical Health

- **Nutrition**: The food you eat or the beverages you drink have a direct impact on your emotions as well as your performance. A well-balanced meal that is made up of fruits, vegetables, lean meats, and healthy fats helps in nourishing the body and the brain. Refraining from the consumption of processed foods and sugary beverages can go a long way in increasing one's energy levels and healthy living.

- **Exercise**: Physical exercise is very vital for the body to be healthy at all times. It doesn't have to be an aggressive exercise; a simple walk in the morning contributes to a better mood and energy levels. Physical activity relieves stress, enhances sleep, and builds up your heart, muscles, and bones.

- **Sleep**: Good sleep is one of the fundamental aspects of our physical well-being. This is the time when your body heals, memory is strengthened, and the body is built up for the next day's activities. Adults should sleep for 7-9 hours per night and establish practices that help them wind down and sleep well.

- **Water**: Water is an essential part of everyone's diet and it is very important to take it in the right proportion. Water is used in the digestive system as an aid in digestion and also in the absorption of nutrients as well as in the regulation of body temperature. Try to consume at least 8 glasses of water per day to ensure that your body and all its organs are in their best shape.

- **Regular Check-ups**: People should go for check-ups now and then and this will help in identifying some health complications early. Screening and vaccinations are an important part of the strategy of preventive measures to prevent diseases in the future. Ensure that you go for check-ups as often as you can, even if you do not have any symptoms.

Mental Health

- **Mindfulness and Meditation**: It is worth mentioning that the mind also requires attention, just like the body. Meditation and similar activities have been known to make an individual more conscious and aware of their surroundings, decrease their level of worry, and increase their concentration levels. Just five to ten minutes of deep breathing or even quiet thinking each day can help immensely.

- **Continuous Learning**: Continuous learning and keeping the mind active helps in improving mental health. Whether it is reading books, solving puzzles, or taking up a new hobby, it is healthy for the brain and prevents one from being bored.

- **Stress Management**: Stress management is very important in the overall well-being of an individual. Some useful strategies include prioritization, setting personal boundaries, and asking for assistance if overwhelmed. Please do not forget that it is acceptable to decline and protect your health.

- **Digital Detox**: Reducing screen time or, rather, limiting the use of gadgets can have a very positive impact on the mind. Excessive screen time causes information overload and stress, which can be detrimental to an individual. Spend some hours in a day without using technology and be involved in other activities.

- **Creativity**: Listening to music, painting, writing a story, or even playing an instrument can help the brain and give one a break from normal daily activities. Creativity helps in the development of problem-solving skills and is a good way to deal with emotions.

Emotional Health

- **Self-awareness**: The first step that is very crucial in the management of emotions is to acknowledge them. Emotional intelligence entails being fully aware of their emotions and how they respond to them so that they can manage their reactions appropriately. It is healthy to vent, so journaling or talking to a close friend can be a good way to get this done.

- **Healthy Relationships**: Staying with positive people can go a long way in improving the general health of an individual. Love is an important need that offers one the feeling of being wanted, chances to turn to when in need, and moments of happiness and fun.

- **Self-Compassion**: Kindness is something that should be practiced towards oneself as well. Self-compassion is the ability to be kind to oneself as one would be to a close friend. It includes practices such as apologizing to oneself, acknowledging successes, and focusing on the self's emotional welfare.

- **Gratitude**: Cultivating thankfulness can help reframe from a scarcity mindset to an abundance mindset. Writing down things that you are grateful for in a gratitude diary or merely focusing on the positive things in life may enhance your mood and make you a happier person.

- **Emotional Expression**: Essentially, it is a good thing to be able to talk things out, write about them, or even draw or paint out your feelings. Suppressing emotions can result in stress and even emotional issues.

Integrating Emotional, Mental, and Physical Health

- **Holistic Approach**: Wellness is a state of overall health that encompasses the physical, mental, and emotional aspects of life. All the pillars are interrelated and complement each other to ensure the achievement of the intended goals. For instance, exercise (physical health) can help you become happier (emotional health) and increase your concentration level (mental health).

- **Routine and Consistency**: Scheduling activities that would fit into the three domains can help in developing a healthy lifestyle. This way, all the aspects of your health are given equal attention and are developed concurrently.

- **Listening to Your Mind and Body**: Stress awareness means recognizing both your body cues and your mental status. If you are tired, stressed, or feel that an emotional toll is being taken on you, then it is most likely that one of the pillars requires attention. Synchronize your schedule to attend to the above needs effectively.

Setting Realistic Health Goals

Realistic health objectives are critical to the process of establishing sustainable lifestyle changes in the pursuit of improved health. This is where planning comes in because it is quite easy to get carried away with the idea of implementing radical changes. Goals should be realistic and have more to do with your situation in particular so that you can make progress without necessarily being pressured.

Your Starting Point

- **Self-Assessment**: As a first step towards developing health goals, one should evaluate his/her current state of health. This encompasses your body's fitness, eating, psychological, and social well-being. Where you are coming from gives you the yardstick by which you can judge your progress or lack of it.

- **Consulting Professionals**: Consult with your doctor, nutritionist, or fitness trainer for the best advice on your diet. They can take into consideration your unique health status and advise you on what you should aim at. Getting professional help means that your goals are protected and are within your health needs.

- **Setting Baselines**: Set health goals for parameters like weight, blood pressure, cholesterol levels, and mental health. These baselines will assist you in the determination of progress and modification of goals in the process of implementation.

Creating SMART Goals

- **Specific**: For your health goals to be effective, they should be well-defined or stated. Instead of the goal to 'get fit,' define a specific goal such as 'walk for 30 minutes daily.' Specific goals give direction and help make decisions on how to achieve them.

- **Measurable**: Make sure that goals are quantifiable so that you can assess the success. For instance, rather than having a general idea like 'eat better,' it would be more effective to have goals like 'take five servings of vegetables per day.' That is why measurable goals are effective in that you can witness the changes and keep the motivation going.

- **Achievable**: The goals should be realistic but at the same time, should be a little difficult to achieve. When the goals set are not achievable, then it results in frustration and high chances of the employees giving up. If you are a layman and you have no prior exercise regime, it would be unwise to aspire to run a marathon in a month. Use a starting point such as, 'walk three times a week' and build up the level of difficulty.

- **Relevant**: You should always ensure that your goals are in line with the general health objective that you have in mind. If your main goal is to enhance the health of your cardiovascular system, then your goals should be along the lines of aerobic exercise. Relevance is important to be able to stay on track and, therefore, to maximize the chances of success.

- **Time-Bound**: Goals should be accompanied by time within which you should be able to accomplish them. This creates more focus and puts more pressure on the actions one has to take. For example, instead of setting a goal such as "lose weight," you should set a goal like "lose 5 pounds in two months." The use of a time frame adds a certain amount of pressure and helps to measure the goals that you have achieved.

Dividing Goals into Smaller Achievable Targets

- **Small Steps**: Divide the long-term goals into achievable sub-goals. This makes goals less of a challenge and more of an accomplishment that can easily be achieved. For example, if you plan to exercise more, begin with one small change at a time, such as increasing the portions of vegetables in your daily meals.

- **Daily and Weekly Milestones**: To keep the motivation high, establish daily and weekly goals. If your target is to gain more physical activity, your daily goal could be a 10-minute walk, and your weekly goal could be to perform a 30-minute workout session. These are the achievements that will help to remain focused and continue the performance.

- **Tracking Progress**: Write down your progress in a notebook or use a health diary or a special application for your smartphone. Writing down the goals, the problems faced and the changes made is useful as it keeps the goal in sight and also provides an overview. Tracking also enables other changes to be made after certain intervals to ensure that the goals are achieved.

Adjusting Goals as Needed

- **Flexibility**: Be open and ready to change the objectives if necessary. Life is dynamic, and people experience changes in their circumstances at one point in their lives. In the case of an injury that hinders running, then opt for other engaging exercises that do not affect the injury, such as swimming or cycling. Flexibility means that even when something is not going as planned, the process can still go on.

- **Celebrating Small Wins**: Always remember to rejoice over the victories you get, as they are great no matter the size. Praise encourages people to continue with the same line of behavior because they are being encouraged. It is good to reward yourself on completion of a particular goal, for instance, buying a new workout dress or getting a spa.

- **Learning from Setbacks**: This means that any time that you are faced with a problem that you are not able to solve, do not look at it as a failure but as a learning process. Do not be too harsh with yourself if you cannot exercise one day or eat some junk food. Identify the problem that occurred, adjust for it, and continue with the plan. Adaptability is vital in the long run.

Involving a Support System

- **Accountability Partners**: Let your friend, family member, or join a support group know your goals. When people have a partner who can keep them on track and motivate them, the level of dedication and results increases dramatically. Support systems encourage, and the process becomes easier since it is not alone.

- **Professional Support**: Connect with other people, such as personal trainers, nutritionists, or therapists. They can help you by steering you in the right direction, giving you advice, and assisting with problematic situations. Professional support helps you to make sure that you have all the necessary tools to work towards the set goals.

Creating a Supportive Environment

It is the support that forms the basis of a proper and healthy existence in any society. To some, it may simply be a location, but for others, it also includes those in your environment, schedules, and mood. When people are surrounded by conditions favorable to their health, it is easy to overcome stress, maintain the intensity of the actions undertaken, and remain optimistic.

Physical Space

- **Declutter**: A messy environment also affects the mind in the same way as it does the physical environment. Maintaining cleanliness in the places where you relax as well as work can help you to avoid stressing yourself and be more productive. When organizing, begin with a specific space and focus on one area for a certain amount of time before moving to another space.

- **Personalize Your Space**: Make sure that objects that you see every day are those that make you happy and that make you feel safe. That means people's portraits, paintings, and souvenirs from trips can help to make the atmosphere cozier and more inspiring.

- **Natural Light and Fresh Air**: Make sure that the environment is very bright and well-ventilated to allow ample air circulation. Daylight improves the mood and people's activity, and the fresh air has a positive impact on the brain and the whole organism. The internal environment of a home should be fresh; open windows often and think of having some plants at home.

- **Comfortable Furniture**: Ensure that the furniture that is to be used in the office is comfortable as well as ergonomic. Correct furniture arrangement can help to avoid musculoskeletal disorders, while comfortable armchairs and sofas can help to take a break. Focus on comfort to develop an area that you would like to be in most of the time.

Emotional Atmosphere

- **Positive Affirmations**: Find and print positive affirmations and motivational quotes and place them around your working area. Such reminders can help to cheer you up and get you in the right mood for positive thinking. Use words and phrases that you prefer.

- **Mindful Colors**: Do not use colors that make the viewer drowsy but those that help in concentration. Pale blue and green can be very soothing, while yellows and oranges can help to energize the room and stimulate creativity. Try out the various shades and identify what works for you.

- **Soothing Sounds**: Try to introduce some elements of sounds that can help you calm down. From smooth melodies to bird chirping to white noise machines, these auditory features can make the environment relaxing and decrease stress levels.

- **Aromatherapy**: Use aromatherapy which involves the use of essential oils to help in establishing a peaceful atmosphere. Essential oils that have calming effects include lavender, chamomile, and eucalyptus since they have positive impacts on the body. These fragrances should be spread through diffusers or candles in the area where they are going to be used.

Social Connections

- **Supportive Relationships**: Build friendships with people who will encourage you and help you in times of need. Always be with people who help you become a better person and who support your healthy lifestyle. Avoid the people who bring you down and make your life miserable, those who take away your energy and will to live.

- **Community Involvement**: This is a good way of creating positive relationships with the people in your society. Being a member of a club, organization, or group helps one to feel wanted and have a sense of duty to perform. These connections can provide comfort and build a sense of belonging in people's lives.

- **Open Communication**: Engage in healthy communication with the people around you. Say what you want, be assertive, and teach others how to be assertive, too. Effective communication enables people to understand each other, hence establishing trust in relationships.

- **Shared Activities**: Engage in activities that you like with other people. No matter whether it is making a meal, going for a run, or discussing something, it can make people feel closer and help them find support in each other.

Routine and Habits

- **Consistent Schedule**: Set a schedule and stick to it, as it should cover working time, free time, and time for the self. It is possible to state that a schedule helps decrease stress as well as provide people with a stable routine. Ensure that you take time to rest in between; do not overwork yourself.

- **Healthy Habits**: Some of the habits that should be adopted include Exercise, a healthy diet, and sleep are some of the basic requirements for the body and mind to be in good health. Develop a schedule that would enable the formation of such habits continually.

- **Mindfulness Practices**: Practice mindfulness activities in your everyday life. Prayer, exercise, yoga, deep breathing, and other techniques will assist a person in staying focused and handling stress. Such practices can be of much value if included in one's working and or daily timetable.

- **Goal Setting**: Try to establish goals that are realistic and attainable to ensure that you do not experience failure. It helps to divide a large goal into smaller ones because the bigger picture becomes less overwhelming when divided into smaller parts. Rejoice in the achievements made throughout the process to remain focused on the goal and maintain a positive outlook.

Chapter 12

Empowering Yourself

Empowering yourself is one of the most fulfilling experiences in life, and it all begins with that first move. It is about being empowered to find your strength and knowledge to make sense of the wellness world. Each decision you make throughout your life, each action that becomes a habit, affects your health and well-being.

Self-empowerment is an effective way to change from being a passive passenger in your own life and becoming an active participant in it. This journey is not for the faint of heart, the bored or the disinterested. It is for those who will dedicate themselves to the self. Now, let it go deeper into how you can use the power within you to attain the kind of health that is worth striving for.

Becoming Your Own Health Advocate

Your Body

Being informed about your body is the first step towards being an advocate for your health. Be aware of your state, your body, and your mind. Record any alterations, even if they are minor ones. This awareness aids in recognizing signs of potential health problems and being able to express them to medical professionals.

- **Listen to Your Body**: Ladies and gentlemen, your body speaks through symptoms. Dizziness, pain, and nausea are some of the signs. Don't ignore them. Recording your progress in a health journal can also be of help in identifying certain patterns and causes.

- **Educate Yourself**: Take time to know your body and other easily diagnosable diseases. Knowledge of basic anatomy and physiology helps ask better questions and makes medical advice easier to comprehend. Newspapers, magazines, other credible online sources, and books are some of the best places to start from.

- **Trust Your Intuition**: You can rely on your feelings that tell you about your health. It is always good to consult another doctor if you feel that something is not right. Listening to your gut feeling is a good thing because it allows for early identification of problems.

Gathering Information

Health advocacy begins with information or the lack thereof. Knowledge is power, and the more one is informed, the better positioned he is to make good decisions.

- **Research Conditions and Treatments**: If there is any disease that is diagnosed then it should be studied fully. Learn about the risk factors, signs, and signs of the disease, as well as the methods of treatment. Having this information will enable you to engage in informative discussions with your healthcare provider.

- **Understand Medications**: Being knowledgeable of the medications you are taking and their purpose is important. Take note of side effects and interactions that may occur. The best source of medication information is pharmacists.

- **Stay Updated**: Health information is dynamic which is why it is imperative to regularly update the knowledge base. Get to know the current knowledge on the issue. Reading through health newsletters or following various health organizations can help you stay updated.

Communicating Effectively

Maintain an open line of communication with your healthcare provider. This makes sure that you get the best treatment as a patient.

- **Be Clear and Concise**: When talking with the doctor about your symptoms or things you are worried about, do not beat around the bush. Make a list of questions and concerns you have before the appointment so that you do not forget them when you are in front of the doctor. This way, you are sure to have captured all the important aspects.

- **Ask Questions**: Do not be shy to ask questions. Observe any uncertainties about your diagnosis, the available treatment plans, and your condition's outlook. It is crucial to have a clear picture of your health so that you can make the right decisions.

- **Document Conversations**: Make it a point to jot down something that was discussed during your appointments. This helps remind you of some details that your healthcare provider may have told you and also helps in ensuring that you adhere to all the instructions given by your healthcare provider.

Building a Support System

Family and friends can also help with your health advocacy endeavors. Choose friends and associates who are supportive of your health improvement process.

- **Friends and Family**: Tell your health story to close ones and loved ones. This can be in the form of words of encouragement and even in the form of assistance in one way or the other.

- **Support Groups**: Another avenue to get support is through support groups that are formed by people who are going through similar health issues. Listening to others or sharing what one has gone through may be very encouraging.

- **Healthcare Team**: Make a healthcare team that you can rely on. This encompasses your general practitioner, medical specialists, and other practitioners that you may be attending to. Cohesive teamwork is likely to offer a one-stop solution to the patient.

Taking Control of Your Health

The best way to become an advocate for yourself is by being proactive when it comes to your health. This entails making choices that will enhance one's health status or quality of life.

- **Healthy Lifestyle**: A proper diet and exercise will solve most of the health problems. This ranges from proper nutrition, exercise, sleep, and the ability to control stress.

- **Preventive Care**: It is important to get routine check-ups and screenings. Preventive care will help to identify any possible health problems in their early stage hence, easily manageable.

- **Manage Chronic Conditions**: If you are diagnosed with a chronic disease, consult your doctor to ensure proper control of the disease. Compliance with treatment regimens and management of lifestyle changes are also important.

Overcoming Barriers

There are always some issues that you may experience when advocating for your health. That is why it is crucial to be ready to cope with these barriers.

- **Financial Constraints**: Some healthcare services can be costly. There should be a search for materials and services that could help in decreasing expenses. Most cultures have accessible and cheap healthcare services available to the people.

- **Healthcare Access**: Health care can be defined in terms of location and/or availability. Telehealth services can be a good substitute in such a case to receive care from the comfort of your home.

- **Navigating the Healthcare System**: Often, the healthcare system is not easy to understand. Never feel uncomfortable to seek assistance when it comes to it. Patient advocates and social workers can help out and give advice.

Finding a Qualified Healthcare Practitioner

Identifying Your Needs

The first step in the process of selecting a competent healthcare provider is making a distinct choice of a health concern. This would help in the search as you would know what you need to be delivered.

- **Specialization**: Consider whether you need a GP or a specialist. For instance, if you have a specific condition like diabetes, a specialist in endocrinology would be more suitable.

- **Type of Care**: Check what kind of care you require. This could include routine check-ups, vaccinations, management of acute episodes of a chronic illness, etc. Identifying this helps in choosing the right practitioner that will assist in achieving the desired health status.

- **Personal Preferences**: Consider our individual needs and wants. Would you like a practitioner who applies global methods? Or somebody who depends on the orthodox kind of medicine? Knowing your preferences can help point you in the right direction.

Researching Potential Practitioners

Once you know what you need the next process is to search the possible healthcare providers. This entails the collection of data as well as assessing their credentials.

- **Credentials and Experience**: Seek out professionals with the right certifications and relevant experience. Their experience in the field can be determined by their board certifications and number of years in practice. Cross-check with the professional body or the board that regulates the profession.

- **Reputation and Reviews**: Read reviews and ratings of people who have undergone the treatment. Of course, it is unlikely that every practitioner will not have some negative feedback at some point; however, if the majority of the comments are positive, then this is also positive. On the other hand, Negative comments that are made severally are suspect.

- **Referrals and Recommendations**: Referrals from other professionals such as doctors. Word of mouth, either from friends, family, or your doctor, can help give recommendations. Recommendations from other healthcare professionals can also be very useful.

Evaluating Compatibility

Choosing a competent healthcare provider is not just about his or her credentials. The relationship between you and the practitioner is very important for the success of the care.

- **Communication Style**: Assess how effectively they communicate. Are they attentive to your complaints and are they able to provide clear elaboration? Effective communication keeps the patient informed and ensures that he or she trusts the health and treatment decisions made.

- **Approach to Care**: Look at their attitude to the patients. Are you consulted on matters of decisions that are to be made? Do they have the willingness to talk about other forms of treatment? A practitioner who understands your decisions and preferences and then involves you in your care plan is the best.

- **Availability and Accessibility**: Make sure that the practitioner is available at the right time that you need him/her. Are you able to schedule appointments? Are they available for an emergency? Maintenance requires easy access and easy reach.

Initial Consultation

A first appointment is a good chance to evaluate a healthcare practitioner. This meeting helps in establishing whether they are the right fit for you or not.

- **Prepare Questions**: Make a list of questions to ask the specialist during consultation. Ask them about their encounter with your particular condition, their management approach, and their crisis management plans.

- **Assess Comfort Level**: Be aware of how comfortable you are during the consultation. Trust your instincts. If you have a comfortable feeling and are confident about them taking care of your pet, it could mean that they are the best.

- **Review Their Responses**: Assess their answers to your questions. Are they detailed and easy to comprehend? Are they willing to go out of their way to listen to your complaints? Their readiness to talk to you is important.

Building a Long-Term Relationship

After identifying a competent healthcare provider, the best approach is to establish continuity. There is evidence to suggest that continuity of care is advantageous to the patient.

- **Regular Appointments**: Make time for simple check-ups and routine procedures. This keeps one healthy and the practitioner can track any changes that may be occurring in the future.

- **Open Communication**: Always keep a good relationship with your practitioner. Inform them about your changes in health and abide by their advice. Transparency helps to guarantee that you get the best of what the healthcare providers can offer.

- **Seek Feedback**: Do not shy off from asking your practitioner for some opinions. Consult them and get to know what they think can be done to enhance your health or treat the conditions you are suffering from. Their advice can be most helpful in your wellness plan.

Navigating Challenges

But even when you have a competent healthcare practitioner, you may face some difficulties. Be ready to face such trials and tribulations.

- **Second Opinion**: If you are not sure of what the doctor is saying or if he has recommended a particular treatment, do not accept it without consulting with another doctor. This is your right as a patient; you are entitled to trust your healthcare choices.

- **Changing Practitioners**: If the relationship with your practitioner is not good, then it is alright to change the practitioner. It is about your health, and fit is crucial.

- **Insurance and Costs**: Make sure the practitioner takes your insurance plan and be specific on the costs to be incurred. Knowing the financial side of the care can help avoid some shocks and also make the care more affordable.

Sharing Your Journey with Others

Telling your story as a patient can be an empowering process and can help people feel connected and inspired. It leads to the opportunity to be understanding and be understood, to establish a sense of belonging that can be so inspiring. When you talk about what you are going through, you not only assist yourself but also offer information and inspiration to people who are going through the same things.

Building a Support Network

- **Connecting with Like-minded Individuals**: Having people around who are in the same boat as you in terms of health goals and struggles fosters a good support system. Whether these are social media groups, local meetings, or online forums, these are important platforms where individuals can find others going through the same experience, get advice, and be encouraged.

- **Family and Friends**: Use your family and friends to help you in your health improvement process. Informing the people around you about what you are going through and the improvements, difficulties, and accomplishments that you encounter helps them be more understanding. They can provide tangible assistance, encouragement, and the element of responsibility.

- **Professional Support**: Interacting with other healthcare professionals like therapists, nutritionists/ dietitians, and fitness trainers/ coaches is beneficial as they are experts. Their experience can assist you in finding your way more efficiently and guarantee that you are making the right choices.

Sharing Your Story

- **Personal Narratives**: There is nothing as encouraging as writing about your health improvement process and seeing yourself improve with each passing day. A blog, social media, or personal journal can help to record one's journey and pass on valuable lessons learned.

- **Public Speaking**: If you feel at ease, then you can go for public speaking to tell your story. This could be during fairs, health awareness crusades, or support groups. Sharing your story can encourage people and create feelings of unity and drive.

- **Visual Storytelling**: Leaving photos, videos, and other types of media to tell your story. This is because visual content is useful in passing emotions and progress, hence making the story feel more real.

Conclusion

Getting to this point in the book, it can be confidently stated that the idea of the wisdom of nature can significantly contribute to the improvement of one's health. With natural remedies, we get back to basics and adopt practices that have been tried and tested and are safe for our use. This trip has been an eye-opener in terms of how ancient wisdom can be blended with modern science in an attempt to offer a wholesome solution to our health problems.

Holistic treatments provide a way to health that is simple and transformative. Whether it is chamomile for sleep, turmeric for inflammation, or countless other examples, nature has endowed us with an enormous array of remedies. But, as we have seen, it is important to tread this route carefully, equipped with the understanding and appreciation of the power of these natural partners.

When you go on with the discovery and implementation of these remedies, do not forget the aspect of responsible use. Get advice from healthcare specialists, remain updated, and never compromise on safety. It is this integration of the knowledge passed down through the ages and the knowledge of the present day that enables people to make choices that are constructive and realistic.

Thank you for going through this discovery process with me. May the information you have received here help and encourage you to live a healthier and happier life.

Appendix

Conversion Charts and Measurements

Volume Conversions

US Standard	Metric Equivalent	Notes
1 teaspoon (tsp)	5 milliliters (ml)	
1 tablespoon (tbsp)	15 milliliters (ml)	
1 fluid ounce (fl oz)	30 milliliters (ml)	
1 cup	240 milliliters (ml)	
1 pint (pt)	473 milliliters (ml)	
1 quart (qt)	946 milliliters (ml)	
1 gallon (gal)	3.785 liters (L)	

Weight Conversions

US Standard	Metric Equivalent	Notes
1 ounce (oz)	28 grams (g)	
1 pound (lb)	454 grams (g)	
1 pound (lb)	0.454 kilograms (kg)	

Length Conversions

US Standard	Metric Equivalent	Notes
1 inch (in)	2.54 centimeters (cm)	
1 foot (ft)	30.48 centimeters (cm)	
1 yard (yd)	0.914 meters (m)	

Temperature Conversions

Fahrenheit (°F)	Celsius (°C)	Conversion Formula
32°F	0°C	(°F - 32) × 5/9 = °C
98.6°F	37°C	(°F - 32) × 5/9 = °C
212°F	100°C	(°F - 32) × 5/9 = °C

Common Herbal Measurements

Measurement	Equivalent	Notes
1 pinch	Approx. 1/8 teaspoon (tsp)	
1 handful	Approx. 1/4 cup	Varies based on hand size
1 sprig	Approx. 1 teaspoon (tsp) chopped.	
1 bunch	Varies	Typically, around 1 cup chopped

Safety Guidelines and Precautions

Natural remedies have to be taken with certain safety measures and precautions, which have to be followed to the letter. Here are essential tips to ensure you use these powerful tools responsibly:

1. **Consult Professionals**: Consult with your healthcare provider before using any herbs for treatment, especially if you are pregnant, breastfeeding, or if you are under some other medications.

2. **Start Slowly**: When introducing new herbal remedies to your diet, you want to do so gradually to track your body's reaction. This makes it easier to note if there are any side effects or allergic reactions that may be caused by the medication.

3. **Research and Verify**: Be sure to get your herbs and supplements from credible and quality producers. Check the correct amount of the supplement and whether it is safe to take it together with other medications.

4. **Be Aware of Interactions**: There are natural remedies that interfere with the working of prescription drugs or cause otherwise damaging effects. Potential interactions should always be looked for.

5. **Follow Dosage Instructions**: Sometimes, too much is not good. Toxicity or side effects can be prevented by following the recommended dosages of the drugs.

6. **Monitor for Allergic Reactions**: Listen to your body. If you see any signs of allergy, such as rashes, swelling, or difficulties in breathing, then stop using the product.

7. **Avoid Self-Diagnosis**: Although there are many natural treatments out there, they do not in any way replace your doctor's consultation and diagnosis.

8. **Educate Yourself**: Be up to date with the herbs that you consume. Knowledge of their properties uses, and side effects prevent adverse effects during the usage.

Following these guidelines can help you utilize the benefits of natural remedies and help you live a healthier and more harmonized life.

Printed in Great Britain
by Amazon

56944737R00057